THE VAGRANT LOTUS
AN INTRODUCTION
TO BUDDHIST PHILOSOPHY

Books by

DOUGLAS A. FOX

Published by The Westminster Press

The Vagrant Lotus:
  An Introduction to Buddhist Philosophy

Buddhism, Christianity,
  and the Future of Man

THE
VAGRANT LOTUS

AN INTRODUCTION
TO BUDDHIST PHILOSOPHY

by
DOUGLAS A. FOX

THE WESTMINSTER PRESS
Philadelphia

Published by The Westminster Press ®
Philadelphia, Pennsylvania

PRINTED IN THE UNITED STATES OF AMERICA

Library of Congress Cataloging in Publication Data

Fox, Douglas A., 1927–
   The vagrant lotus: an introduction to Buddhist philosophy.
   Bibliography: p.

   1. Buddhist doctrines—Introductions.   2. Philosophy, Buddhist. I. Title.
BQ4132.F69   294.3′4′2   73–8692
ISBN 0–664–20975–0
ISBN 0–664–24979–5 (pbk.)

For Margaret

CONTENTS

Preface   11

Part One: HISTORICAL PROLEGOMENA

   I.   The Buddha: The Man, the Message,
        and the Myth   15

  II.   The Vagrant Lotus   37

Part Two: BUDDHIST PHILOSOPHY

 III.   Buddhism: Religion or Philosophy?   49

 IV.   The Nature of Reality
        and the Ground of Value   65

  V.   Man and His Existence   113

 VI.   The Way and the Wayfarers   145

Notes   205
Bibliography   213
Index   217

PREFACE

In recent years Buddhism has become a subject of considerable interest in Europe and America. Despite this, most introductions to Buddhist thought are fragmentary, in that they deal with only one of the two great divisions of the tradition, Theravāda or Mahāyāna, or they are so apologetic and enthusiastic in nature as to obscure the problems that philosophy should recognize and discuss. The present book is intended to present the reader with a sympathetic but critical discussion of *both* Theravāda and Mahāyāna Buddhism, and to do so in a manner designed to lead beyond purely preliminary considerations, although demanding no previous acquaintance with the subject.

I should like to acknowledge my indebtedness to Professors Masao Abe, Shojun Bando, and especially Hiroshi Sakamoto, all of whom directed my attention to important issues and sources and the last of whom served as a regular guide and mentor in the intricacies of Buddhist philosophy during a very happy year in Kyoto. Whatever is of value in this book is theirs; whatever is inadequate is most surely mine.

D. A. F.

Colorado Springs

Part One
HISTORICAL PROLEGOMENA

I
THE BUDDHA: THE MAN,
THE MESSAGE, AND THE MYTH

From Uska Bazar, near the Nepal border, to Gaya, south of the Ganges and southeast of Benares, the struggle for life and something more than life has led to the cultivation of many things: sugarcane, tobacco, indigo, and much else to fill the stomach and please the mind. Twenty-five centuries ago a profound disenchantment with the best in life planted there a seed of quite another sort, and out of the confusion of India's innumerable cults and fancies it has thrust forth, as a lotus from a forest bog, a powerfully enduring flower—Buddhism, one of the greatest religious traditions of mankind.

Amid rocky hills which some have found uniquely beautiful and strangely productive of tranquillity, an enigmatic man lived and died, leaving a legacy of ideas which, for all its complexity and even perhaps inner contradiction, has deeply moved men ever since. He has been called the Buddha, the Fully Awakened One, and the curious fact is that we shall never be able to forget him although we shall never be able to know precisely what he was like or even what he said. He moves behind a mist of myth in which he is presented sometimes as a wise man and at other times as a kind of cosmic Ultimate, unborn and undying. What was he, then, and what were the things he taught?

Truth is an unruly spirit, and the truth about the Buddha is that we can no longer hope to extricate fact from fantasy and set before ourselves an image as faithful as a photograph or a verbal record beyond the reach of doubt. Pious imaginations have given us almost all we know of him, and although some of this is probably quite sober stuff, none of the scriptures (in their present form at least) can be safely dated earlier than about 140 years after his death, so that plenty of time for the operation of creative fancy separates the Buddha from the records of his life. By comparing scripture with scripture, by sifting scrupulously, by glaring critically at clamoring data, one may determine a corpus of material which is more likely than the rest to present the Buddha and his words with minimal distortion. After the most careful scrutiny, however, it remains true that what glows with patent authenticity for one man is deeply shadowed by improbability for another. Nevertheless if we take those things which have seemed to a great many people to be more plausible than others, we arrive at a brief and tentative statement such as the one that follows:

BUDDHA: THE MAN AND HIS TEACHING

Around the year 560 B.C., there was born in the ancient city of Kapilavastu a child whose name was to be Siddhartha Gautama (the latter being his family name). His parents were probably wealthy members of the warrior caste and the Sakya clan, and his mother may have died a few days after his birth. He enjoyed (or, like most of us, failed to do so) the usual education of his class and time, but his father took unusual pains to protect him from contact with unpleasantness and suffering. While quite young (perhaps only sixteen years old) he married his cousin, Yasodhara, and about ten years later the couple produced a son whom Siddhartha named Rahula ("the fetter"). Soon thereafter Siddhartha became dissatisfied with the transience and suffering which he saw to be inescapable in life and at about the age of twenty-nine he forsook his small family and the comforts of his home to become a mendicant—a wandering seeker of truth. Especially he wanted to find a way of understanding and, if possible, of overcoming the unpleasant experiences of old age, disease, disappointment, and death. He seems to have studied with at least two notable spiritual masters, but to have left them both when he found their teachings unsatisfactory. He explored the fruits of extreme asceticism and the usual mystical disciplines of his land, but nothing brought him the answers he sought, although temporary peace was a product of some of his mystical attainments.

Finally, after six or seven years of striving, Siddhartha achieved a flash of understanding in which he saw clearly what he regarded as the sufficient and liberating answer to life's riddles, and for the next forty-five years, until his death at the age of eighty, he preached his doctrines with remarkable success. In doing so, he challenged many of the traditional assumptions of Indian religion and philosophy, abandoned their hallowed scriptures and authorities, and decried their rituals.

This, then, is the skeleton which many generations of Buddhists have enfleshed extravagantly. What, with similar austerity, can be said about his teaching?

As we have noted, Gautama clearly regarded himself as in reaction against conventional Indian philosophy and piety. He felt that he had tested in his own experience the ways of Indian mysticism and had found them seriously lacking.[1] Walpola Rahula admirably summarizes what seems to have been the Buddha's point of view when he notes that "all the spiritual and mystic states, however pure and high they may be, are mental creations, mind-made, conditioned and composed [samkhata]. They are not Reality, not Truth [sacca]."[2] Beyond these states lay the truth he had sought, and it is not entirely clear, despite later developments of Buddhist doctrine, that Gautama felt this truth to be utterly beyond verbalization. Certainly it had to be realized intuitively by each individual if it was to become effective in his life, but it might be expressible neatly and quite rationally. The first systematic expression of it seems to have taken the form of an exposition of what came to be known as the Four Noble Truths. Here we find that Buddhist teaching which can, with most confidence, be ascribed to Gautama, since it is so universal among our sources and appears so early in the growth of the tradition. The Dīgha Nikāya, Vol. II, No. XXII, gives us one of the most succinct treatments of this theme. Therefore we shall base the following outline upon it.

THE FOUR NOBLE TRUTHS

The first of the Buddha's Truths is simply that to exist is inescapably to suffer:

And what, bhikkhus, is the Noble Truth of suffering? Birth is suffering, old age is suffering, death is suffering, grief, lamentation, pain, misery and despair are all suffering; not to get what one desires is to suffer. In short, the five aggregates of existence are bound to suffering.[3]

We shall discuss the "aggregates of existence" (Sanskrit: *skandha;* Pali: *khandha*) in Chapter IV. For the moment we need only note that Gautama is teaching here that whatever rises to self-consciousness must expect to endure anguish of various sorts. After all, we and all that we desire or love are impermanent; therefore how could life be other than one disappointment, one frustration, one diminishment after another?

> Did you never see in the world a man or woman, eighty, ninety, or a hundred years old, feeble, crooked as a gabled roof, bent over, propped up with a stick, moving insecurely with tottering steps; someone whose youth has long since fled, whose teeth are broken, whose hair is gone or is grey and thin; someone whose skin is wrinkled and discolored? And when you saw such a person did you never reflect that you, too, cannot possibly escape a similar decay?
>
> Did you never see in the world a man or woman who was seriously ill, wallowing in his own vomit, and who had to be lifted up and set down by other persons? And did you never think that you, too, are vulnerable to disease and cannot forever escape it?
>
> Did you never see in the world the corpse of a man or woman after it has lain for two or three days? A corpse swollen, blue-black in hue and utterly corrupt? And did you not think that you, too, are subject to death without reprieve? [4]

The second of the great Truths is that suffering has its seed in craving or desire:

> And what, bhikkhus, is the Noble Truth of the origin of suffering? Craving, which leads to rebirth, which is associated with lust and self-indulgence, and which seeks its satisfaction in numerous places [is its origin]. [5]

Craving, according to our text, is essentially of three kinds:
sensual desire, desire for eternal existence, and desire for
success, however we define this last. When desire is unsatisfied it yields frustration, and when it is satisfied it leads
to disenchantment, disappointment, and eventual loss. This
is because there is nothing in the world, including ourselves, that endures indefinitely, and desires attach us as
transient beings to other transient things.

The Buddha's third Truth is that suffering can be es-
caped by the elimination of desire:

> And what, bhikkhus, is the Noble Truth about the extinc-
> tion of suffering? It [the extinction of suffering] comes
> from the abandonment of, the destruction of craving, our
> renunciation of it and emancipation and detachment from
> it.[6]

Since suffering, in the broadest sense, is produced by desire, the elimination of desire must eliminate suffering too.
This contention is made more plausible if we remember
that our continued participation in a cycle of rebirths
(which may, in principle, continue indefinitely) is assumed here to be promoted by our clinging to life or to
some perfect state as one form of the pervasive and perni-
cious desire under discussion. Thus, when desire for wealth
is overcome, poverty involves no anguish; when desire for
fame is abandoned, obscurity is no burden, but when desire for either life or the peace of non-life is at last for-
saken, the ultimate release is ours, for this means the
arising of that condition of perfect equilibrium in which
we seek nothing, are disappointed in nothing, and can lose
nothing we shall regret. Further, the very force that drove
the wheel of our repeated involvement in life has been
marvelously brought to naught.[7]

Eightfold Path of Discipline

The fourth and final great Truth concerns the way in which desire can be overcome, and it entails the explication of the Eightfold Path of discipline:

> And what, bhikkhus, is the Noble Truth about the Way that leads to the end of suffering? This is that Noble Eightfold Path, namely, right understanding, right mindedness, right speech, right action, right livelihood, right effort, right attentativeness, right concentration.[8]

A brief explanation of what is meant by each of the steps in this path will be useful, but its full meaning will become clear only after we have discussed many other matters that lie before us. Meanwhile, let us consider each of the steps in turn.

1. *Right Understanding*

This is frequently held to mean simply the understanding of the Four Noble Truths themselves, but the *Majjhima Nikāya* extends this to include a knowledge of which behaviors are meritorious and which earn for us spiritual demerit. The same source offers us the following list of demeritorious actions:

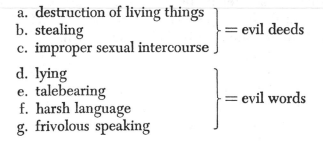

a. destruction of living things
b. stealing   } = evil deeds
c. improper sexual intercourse

d. lying
e. talebearing
f. harsh language   } = evil words
g. frivolous speaking

h. covetousness
i. ill will   } = evil thoughts
j. wrong views

Obviously the contraries of these are meritorious conduct.
What is most important to note here is that Right Understanding has been made to include an understanding of the
content of the second, third, and fourth steps in the
Eightfold Path which, therefore, cannot be taken with any
hope of success until this first one is sufficiently mastered.

2. Right Mindedness

This means the cultivation of thoughts quite free from
covetousness, ill will, egotistical stubbornness, or any other
elements conducive to demeritorious behavior. Lust, de-
lighted reflections upon cruelty, and so on must also therefore be eliminated and the mind must seek to fill itself with
thoughts of benevolence, purity, and kindness.

3. Right Speech

Rather obviously, this means the avoidance of lying,
talebearing, harsh language, and frivolous talk. It means
speaking with moderation: saying what needs to be said,
but without useless embellishment. Above all, it means
speaking the truth and especially that Truth which the
Buddha made the subject of all his conversation.

4. Right Action

One must avoid killing, stealing, and unlawful sexual
contact. There are complexities here which we shall re-

serve for exploration in Chapter VI, but the general tenor
is reasonably clear.

5. *Right Livelihood*

"When the noble disciple avoids a wrong manner of livelihood and lives by means of a right one, this is called
Right Livelihood."[9] Various sources inform us that a
wrong livelihood may involve trickery, treachery, cajolery,
dissembling, rapacity, and the like, and the *Anguttara
Nikāya* tells us that "five trades should be avoided by a
disciple: trading in arms, in living beings, in flesh, in intoxicants, and in poison."[10]

6. *Right Effort*

There are four great "efforts" which a faithful Buddhist
should strive to expend: the effort to avoid the arising of
evil within himself or without; the effort to overcome evil;
the effort to develop good conditions; the effort to maintain the good that exists.

7. *Right Attentiveness*

This is a fundamental, and in some respects unique,
facet of the Buddha's teaching and it refers to the cultivation of certain attitudes and skills in meditation. A more
complex version of this step in the Path will be dealt with
in the final chapter, but let us note now that there are four
main elements in Right Attentiveness:

a. Contemplation of the body in order to disabuse ourselves of any illegitimate fondness for it. We note its
transience, the grotesque functions it performs (bowel

movements, chewing and digesting food, and so on), the general unpleasantness of the body's constituents—hair, bones, intestines, stomach, excrement, bile, phlegm, pus, blood, spittle, nasal mucus, and so on. Thus by contemplating the body properly we become aware that it is frail and loathsome. We learn not to wish to be identified with it.

b. Contemplation of emotions. We should study carefully the rising and falling of our various feelings and thus become aware of their extreme instability. Thus we will be able to detach ourselves even from them.

c. Contemplation of the mind. The object of this is, again, detachment and the abandonment of a sense of selfhood. The process includes examining the movement of our mental processes, noting their transience, and learning to stand "outside" them, as it were, so that we do not falsely think of them as constituting a self, stable and secure.

d. Contemplation of phenomena. Consider carefully any and all phenomena that we daily confront: the presence in and around us of anger, lust, anxiety; the elements of material existence; sounds, odors, tastes, ideas, and anything else encountered. Contemplate, too, the Four Noble Truths themselves, and through all this learn to distinguish the transient and the eternal and to become detached from the former.

8. Right Concentration

"Whatever, friend Visakha, is one-pointedness of mind, this is concentration." [11] In other words, the aim here is to fix the attention upon one object only and thus to narrow and deepen awareness instead of allowing it to spill diffusely over the entire landscape of our imagination and perception. This is the road to skill in meditation, and together the last two steps of the Path will lead us to see for ourselves the truth which the Buddha freely proclaims.

Here, then, we have an outline of the basic teaching of the man Gautama. Even this much is probably impossible to state without involuntarily adopting ideas added to his thought by later minds, but we can be reasonably confident that something like the foregoing represents the message he proclaimed. Both the Buddha and his teaching, however, are by now disguised within layer upon layer of speculation and myth, and to this we must next turn.

The Mythical Buddha

To say that the information we have about Gautama is generally mythical is, unfortunately, to suggest to many people that it has the quality of a television commercial. A myth may be quite accurate in its data or it may have no connection with historical events at all, but even in the latter case it is by no means merely a legend or fairy tale.

The term "myth" has been variously used and defined, and to avoid confusion I shall specify as plainly as possible what it means in the present context. A myth is a story that expresses, usually in the mode of event, a conviction that is the foundation of belief and action within a religious tradition, and that often could not be fully encompassed by any other form of expression (for instance, by philosophy). Thus, for example, the stories about Jesus the Christ are Christian "myths," not because they are untrue, but because they are the basis upon which theologians and philosophers speculate and upon which ordinary Christians base their beliefs and actions, and because their "truth" *cannot* entirely be reduced to any other form of expression. One might write a theological explication of these myth

events, but at the end one will not have captured all that
the event itself proclaims or all that it is capable of evok-
ing in the awareness of a faith-full respondent. Myth is,
therefore, not an inferior way of writing history or philosophy but a unique form which complements all others. Indeed, it may be said to be the richest mode of verbal
expression ever evolved by man, for it draws upon the
poetic, philosophical, and mystical imaginations at the
same time.

It must be clear, then, that all attempts to "demy-
thologize" the scriptures of any religion are mistaken in
principle, and so are all tendencies to see the stories as
significant because they are accurate as historical records.
The myth that is most removed from historical facticity
may, indeed, be most profoundly "true," and at least it will
be more important than any mere history if we wish to
understand the meaning of the religious tradition to which
it belongs.

This does not mean that historicity is unimportant. That
a historical man, Jesus of Nazareth, was the concrete act
of God in a specific moment of time is, in my judgment,
indispensable to Christian belief. But what we are saying
is that myths (e.g., the stories *about* Jesus of Nazareth
seen as the Christ) are important aside from their historical accuracy because they express the *meaning* of the historical event which is called "Christ."

In Buddhism, historical fact is less important than it
is in Christianity because the Buddhist view of the significance of particular persons and happenings is quite
different from the Christian. Myth, however, remains important, for it is the path we must tread if we wish to
capture for ourselves the impact made by the Buddha upon
his followers, and if we would understand in some measure

the subsequent meaning of Buddhism for all who have embraced it. We shall have space here only to sample the rich mythology that fills many volumes of Buddhist scripture, but perhaps even that will suffice to give us a deeper appreciation of our subject.

Gautama's life, according to the myths, was the last of hundreds of incarnations through which he had gradually achieved the six perfections required of a Buddha, the perfections of giving, morality, patience, vigor, meditation, and wisdom. There are stories that illustrate his attainment of these perfections, one compact selection of which is contained in Nāgārjuna's second-century commentary on the *Perfection of Wisdom*. (Edward Conze's conveniently arranged little volume entitled *Buddhist Scriptures* gives a succinct selection from this material.)

To illustrate the perfection of giving, we have the story of a former life of the Buddha (when, in fact, he was a certain King Shibi). The good king one day rescued a pigeon from a hawk, but then, to compensate the hawk for its loss, he gave it some of his own flesh to eat. Again the Buddha reveals for us what is meant by the perfection of patience. In one former incarnation a somewhat unpleasant king found the future Buddha in a forest surrounded by all the royal wives. They had, as a matter of fact, discovered the saint there by accident and, being captivated by his wisdom, were clustered around him merely to improve their minds. But the king, who had probably failed to notice that they had minds, thought the sage was usurping certain regal prerogatives and angrily ordered the palace guards to cut off successively his "rival's" hands, arms, ears, nose, and feet. Throughout the entire operation the saint remained perfectly tranquil, without a hint of anger or fear.

With regard to vigor, which means energy of mind and body spent in attaining enlightenment, the Buddha's earlier lives again provide us with examples. Once, for instance, he had praised a former Buddha named Pushya for seven days and nights while standing on one leg with his eyes open and unblinking.

As for meditation, he had long since become master of all the states of trance. When he was a saint named Shankhacarya his trance was so deep on one occasion that his breath ceased to flow. His hair, at that time, was braided and wound like a conch shell, and a bird had laid her eggs in it. When he finally became aware of this, the good man deliberately remained quite motionless until the eggs hatched and the young birds learned to fly.

Thus, many incarnations and many noble accomplishments had prepared the way for the final achievement: Buddhahood itself.

The Jataka Tales tell us[12] that when the time came for him to be born, the future Buddha was in the thirteenth, or highest, heaven. Told by the gods of his destiny, he made what are called the "five surveys": he chose the moment for his birth, the continent and birthplace, the clan, and the persons who should be his father and mother. His father would be King Suddhodana of the Sakya clan, and his mother Queen Maya. It was important to him that his mother should die a few days after his birth (as is traditional with Buddhas) because he wanted to avoid the most entangling of all human relationships.

At the time of a midsummer festival, Queen Maya enjoyed a remarkable dream. In it she saw a *bodhisattva*, or saint, who was now to become her son Siddhartha, enter her right side in the form of a white elephant. Ten months later Siddhartha was born. This occurred when the queen was on her way to visit her parents and was passing near a grove of trees which were miraculously in flower out of season. The child was born from the right side of the queen, and immediately the earth trembled and the gods received the baby in a golden net and personally bathed him. When he was returned to earth the baby stood up, took seven steps, and declared, "I am the greatest of all worldly ones: this is my last existence!"

Naturally enough such a manner of birth raised suspicions about the character of the infant, and these were further stimulated when a soothsayer informed the infant's father that the child's body clearly bore the traditional thirty-two marks of the Great Male and that he would therefore become either a world-conquering monarch or a Buddha. King Suddhodana inclined to the former alternative as an impeccable career for his son, so he planned a program designed to keep Siddhartha from becoming aware of the troubles that afflict our world. He surrounded the lad from birth with every comfort, luxury, and beauty, carefully removing from his environment all evidence of decay.

Despite the king's efforts, the so-called "first miracle" quickly indicated that there were forces at work to frustrate his militaristic intention. This occurred at a plowing festival when the child's nurses had set him under a tree where he could watch what was going on and then wandered off in pursuit of their own interests. The young prince was fascinated as he watched the plowing, but he noticed that as the soil was turned over, worms and larvae were exposed and instantly devoured by enthusiastic birds. Alas, the very birds who had just glutted themselves were thereupon attacked in turn and eaten by falcons. Siddhartha was overcome with pity at this sight, and when his nurses remembered him, rather belatedly, and returned several hours after leaving him beneath the tree, they found him sitting cross-legged and in a trance. And the shadow of the tree, in defiance of the moving earth, remained where it had been in the morning, still protecting him from the hot sun.

At last the gods decided to take a hand in the education of the prince. They were afraid that King Suddhodana's plan might work, and Siddhartha might be diverted toward a career of world conquest, so they planned a curriculum which would instruct the young man in the impermanence and untrustworthiness of all earthly triumphs. When he was about twenty-nine years old, the gods confronted Siddhartha with four signs. The story concerning them is one of the best known in Buddhist literature.

Knowing that he could hardly keep his son housebound forever (this, after all, being no way to win a world), King Suddhodana gave permission for Siddhartha to go on sight-seeing trips outside the palace grounds. But he first prepared the route carefully, ordering that every indication of distress be rigorously kept away from the streets along which the prince's carriage would pass. Thus all beggars, all aged or sick persons, were kept away from the route. But on the first of these expeditions one of the gods, disguised as an ancient and decrepit man, suddenly appeared near the royal vehicle. Siddhartha was astonished and asked his charioteer to explain this unprecedented sight. The faithful servant replied that it was no unusual thing which the prince was seeing, but merely an example of old age—a fate that awaited all men.

On successive trips Siddhartha saw a diseased person, a corpse, and finally a monk who appeared serene despite his obvious poverty. As the first three of these visions dis-

tressed Gautama enormously, the last made him wonder
whether the answers to the questions arising in his mind
were not to be found in a monkish and meditative life
rather than in a palatial one.

On the night of the full moon in May came the event
known as the Great Renunciation. Gautama awoke to the
sound of heavenly voices urging him to leave his home
and become a wandering seeker of truth. He glanced
around him and saw his palace dancing girls lying asleep
in disgusting attitudes and it suddenly seemed to him that
his palace was a cemetery of decomposing bodies. The
prince stole one last look at his sleeping wife and child,
awakened his faithful charioteer, and set off. He rode to a
grove of trees where a band of hermits were known to live,
and then dismissed his servant and his horse, sending them
home. The horse, however, was brokenhearted at thus part-
ing forever from his master and lay down to die.

Next came six or seven years of strenuous ascetic and
meditational striving. He joined five other monks (the
most severely ascetic he could find) and lived with them
in the forest of Uruvilva near Bodh Gaya. The excessive
deprivations which they encouraged him to practice, however, undermined his health until one day he fainted help-
lessly. When he awoke he reflected that asceticism had
merely weakened him and had actually made it more difficult for him to think clearly or to concentrate his attention
for long periods. So he renounced asceticism and was
thereupon himself renounced and deserted by his five
former colleagues.

Soon Gautama became aware, through a number of supernatural signs, that a great moment was near, so as night
fell he sat under a tree (called in retrospect the Bodhi
tree—"tree of enlightenment") and, facing east, made his

famous vow: "Let my skin, sinews and bones become dry, and the flesh and blood in my body dry up! But I will never stir from this seat without having realized supreme enlightenment."

Now, Mara, the Evil One, was alarmed by Gautama's determination. He feared that the monk might attain a vision of truth and thereafter manage to achieve a great deal of good in the world—a prospect not to be contemplated with equanimity by any responsible fiend. Therefore Mara began to hurl whirlwinds, showers of stones, burning coals, and other missiles at Gautama, and threatened him with even more tiresome antics. But all was to no avail. So Mara changed his tactics. He sent his three nymph daughters (representing respectively sexual love, seduction, and infatuation) to seduce Siddhartha, but he exerted magical power to transform them into hags.

At last Gautama entered into profound meditation and during the night broke through all barriers into a state of perfect enlightenment. He possessed full knowledge of his former existences, had the power of supernatural perception, and saw clearly the whole process of cause and effect which constitutes the nature of existence. He had now become the Buddha. He knew what caused suffering and what could cure it; he knew that he was forever free from the need to exist again in another human form. He sang a great victory song:

> Seeking the builder of the house
> I have spun my way in the wheel
> Of countless births, never escaping pain.
> Suffering comes in birth after birth!
> House Builder, you are seen!
> Never a house shall you build for me again!
> All your tackle is shattered;

> The roof beam is a splintered ruin.
> The elements of Mind are scattered
> And desire's death is reached.[13]

Mara now played his last card. He argued persuasively that Gautama, having won his deliverance, should gather immediately his full reward, slipping unobtrusively from the troubled social scene into the endless and passionless peace of perfect *Nirvāna*. Why, after all, should he stay in the world? To help men? But how could that be done? Men are like lotus bulbs planted in a palace pond: some are strong enough to grow and blossom, needing no gardener, and others will never flourish, no matter what is done for them.

At this point the gods were alarmed and one of their number came to argue with Mara before Gautama. It is true, the deity conceded, that there are men who need no help and men who cannot be helped. But there is also a third class; men who cannot flourish alone, but who can be cultivated. The Buddha saw the justice of this and agreed to remain with mankind to spread his knowledge.

The new Buddha next went toward the city of Benares and found near there, in a place called the Deer Park, his five erstwhile comrades and preached to them his first sermon, traditionally entitled "The Turning of the Wheel of the Law." He converted all five of them, and in the ensuing months conversions continued to occur until he had sixty disciples. All these were sent out to preach the doctrines of the new Faith, thus establishing at the very outset of its career the missionary orientation of Buddhism. The Master's words were: "Go, monks, preach the Noble Doctrine. . . . Let no two of you go in the same direction." [14]

Thus began the Buddha's ministry, and it lasted for forty-five successful years until his death. The first twenty of these years he spent wandering and preaching in many places of his region, but during the last twenty-five he generally remained in monasteries near Sravasti, allowing the multitudes to come to him there.

Late in his life Gautama had to face the question of whether or not to establish an order of nuns to complement that of the monks. At first he refused, having apparently a rather dim view of women. Indeed, he is supposed to have discussed women with his friend and disciple Ananda once, and to have said that women are easily angered, passionate, envious, and stupid, and therefore ought to be excluded from public assemblies. Whether this story is true or a mere canard (possibly attributable to a male chauvinist of a later time!), it would seem that a meditational order for women succeeded that of the men. Again there is a familiar story: On the day before his death Gautama's stepmother, Mahaprajapati, came to him and begged for permission to found an order. He was at first reluctant, but softened at last and agreed. As the lady went happily on her way, the Buddha confided to Ananda that since women had now received permission to be ordained, the pure religion could not endure for its full span. In fact he predicted, it is said, that in its purity and strength it would survive for a mere five hundred years instead of the thousand it would otherwise have flourished.

At the age of eighty the Buddha died near Kusinagara. The scriptures say that the first symptoms of his fatal illness appeared a little before the actual time of his death, but he suppressed them, since he did not want to die before taking leave of his disciples. At any rate, in a small village named Papa he had a meal with the local smith, a man named Cunda. Apparently the food was poisoned (there are various traditions; some say it was bad pork, others a poisonous mushroom. The question is academic) and after tasting it Gautama asked Cunda to serve something else to his disciples. He, however, ate what had been set before him.

Immediately after he had eaten he began to suffer intense pain. He rested for a while and then crossed a river to a grove of trees which, like those around him at his birth, were flowering out of season. There he spent the last hours of his life. They were busy hours, as he preached to the gathering disciples and specified the four sites that were to be the chief places of Buddhist pilgrimage: the Bodhi tree at Bodh Gaya, the Deer Park near Benares, his birthplace, and the place of his death.

During the night the Buddha gave his disciples one final invitation to ask of him anything that would resolve remaining doubts concerning the teaching he had brought, but they had no uncertainties left. He had assumed the Lion's Position (lying on his side with his head supported by his right hand, a position used in Buddhist art to represent *Nirvāna*) and spoke his last words: "Now, then, O Monks, I tell you: transitory are all composite things; work out your salvation with diligence." [15] Then he entered the various stages of trance and finally died, thereby attaining the perfection of *Nirvāna* which has no psychophysical residue.

This has been a mere outline of the mythical data concerning Gautama Buddha. As the years passed, that data grew richer and more obviously devotional in flavor, and the Buddha as an enlightened man seemed to recede in favor of a more mysterious and virtually divine entity. But never was he *merely* a divinity. Rather, he stood as far

above the gods as they above the jungle's apes. The
Kevaddha Sutta, a Pali scripture, tells a story with which
we shall end this chapter.

A monk was one day puzzled by a metaphysical prob-
lem and went to consult the great god Brahma, whom he
found in the company of a considerable celestial retinue.
Patiently Brahma listened to the monk's question: "Where
do the elements cease and leave no trace?" Brahma replied,
"I am the Great Brahma, the Supreme, the Mighty, the
All-seeing, the Ruler, the Lord of All, the Controller, the
Creator, the Chief of All, appointing to each his place, the
Father of all that are and that are to be."

"Yes," said the monk, "but I did not ask you what you
are; I asked where the four elements cease and leave no
trace." Then Brahma drew the importunate monk aside
where they could talk privately and said: "These gods
think I know everything. That's why I did not answer your
question in front of them. The fact is, I cannot answer you.
You had better go and ask the Buddha." [16]

II

THE VAGRANT LOTUS

A supreme symbol of Buddhism is the lotus, for the image
of this exquisite flower rising in its growth from the mud
and murk of a pond to rest, at last, in sunlight is suggestive
of the Buddhist's quest. He, too, strives to surmount the
darkness of illusion and to break into the light of perfect
understanding when he shall become a fragrance to purify
the fetid vapors of this world. And the lotus may serve
as a symbol not only of the Buddhist and his enlightenment, but of Buddhism itself. In the next few pages we
shall try to sketch the pattern of its growth.

Very soon after the Buddha's death his followers began to dispute the correctness of various interpretations of
his teachings. These controversies were probably intensified by local influences as the Faith began to spread and
encounter a wider range of alien ideas. At any rate, a dis-
puted but fairly strong tradition holds that within the very
year of Gautama's final entry into *Parinirvāna* (that is, in
the year of his death) a council of five hundred monks was
assembled at Rājagrha, the Magadhan capital, to attempt
a consensus on the Master's meaning. Schism, however,
continued and grew wider, for, in the absence of the Buddha himself, there never was a central authority with

37

enough prestige to command the loyalty of all Buddhists.
Instead, the monastic community, the *sangha,* was splin-
tered into many more or less autonomous local institutions
and the relations between many of them became extremely
tenuous as Buddhism extended itself geographically.

A century after the "First Council" a second is said to
have met at Vaiśālī, and at this time the irreversible nature
of division within the household of Buddhist Faith became
clear. A strenuous debate occurred concerning matters
of monastic discipline, and two clearly defined parties
emerged. One of these—the smaller, but by no means the
less energetic or eloquent—claimed to sustain the teaching and authority of the Buddha's own immediate disciples
and this group formed the seed of the eventual Theravāda
("Way of the Elders") school. Their rivals, the Mahāsang-
hikas ("Great Assemblists"), argued for a more liberal
interpretation of the rules of life, and for the authority of
the entire contemporary assembly of monks. Very probably
we see here the beginning of the later Mahāyāna movement.

Unfortunately division did not remain as simple as its
pristine form. Quite soon, the tradition tells us, there were
as many as eighteen "schools" of Buddhist thought and
each of these was busily preparing its own canon of scriptures and its own system of interpretation. The Lotus at
this point begins to behave like a schizophrenic dandelion
scattering seeds with splendid abandon. Yet this much may
be said for its coherence: so far as one can see, all of the
eighteen early schools teach what has been justly termed
a "radical pluralism" of transient ontological elements.
Their world, that is to say, is constructed of innumerable
brief atomlike particles (both material and immaterial)
and the chief intellectual business of the schools was the

gradual evolving of a systematic explanation of the relations and careers of these elements—the so-called *abhidharma* (Pali: *abhidhamma*) speculation. Of this we shall have much more to say in Chapter IV.

Not all the energies of the early schools were spent in speculation or controversy, however. From the beginning, Buddhism had a powerful missionary impulse and its teaching was conveyed, in the first centuries, by mendicant monks. Virtually nothing is known about the details of this early expansion, but it may safely be assumed to have followed the principal trade routes from Bihar into the adjoining states. Its progress at this time would seem to have been unspectacular, but no doubt it was steady.

In 326 B.C., the indefatigable (but, as events were soon to prove, entirely mortal) Alexander the Great launched his northwest India adventure and left in his wake some small states with Greek or at least Hellenized rulers. Possibly to his posthumous chagrin he managed to influence the development of Buddhism very little at first, but the seed he planted slowly bore fruit, so that in time the art of Buddhism and probably some of its ideas owed significant texture to Hellenistic inspiration.

Of more importance for our story, however, was the arising, in about 320 B.C., of a new and vigorous dynasty in Magadha. The founder was a certain Chandragupta of the Maurya clan, and he initiated the great Maurya empire which at last (under his successors) included almost all of the Indian peninsula and Afghanistan. One of Chandragupta's descendants was the emperor Asoka, and with this man a new chapter in the growth of Buddhism began.

Asoka opened his kingly career in the style to which his illustrious predecessors had become accustomed, expand-

ing his influence to new horizons by efficient military procedures. It would seem, however, that he was revolted by
the horror of the slaughter he had effected in overcoming
Kalinga, and in the ninth year of his reign he recoiled from
militarism, vowing to conquer henceforth only in the
power of the *dharma*. Such conquests, he tells us, will
create peace and happiness.

It has often been suggested that Asoka's *dharma* was
identical with the doctrinal content of Buddhism or of
some particular sect of Buddhism, but this is probably to
assume too much. *Dharma* may mean simply "righteous
order" and Asoka may have meant little more than that he
would recommend himself as a ruler by the justice and
wisdom of his system of government. Nevertheless it is
clear from various inscriptions he has left us that Buddhism did inform his thinking and (despite frequent statements in textbooks) that although neither he nor anyone
else ever made Buddhism the "official" or "established" religion of India, under him it certainly did flourish to an
unprecedented degree, capturing the allegiance of vast
numbers of persons. Asoka's own religious convictions
would seem, to judge from inscriptions, to have been quite
simple. There are important Buddhist ideas (for instance,
Nirvāna) to which he makes no reference; but he stresses
the importance of morality and attacks, in true Buddhist
fashion, superstition and ceremony. Under Asoka's patron-
age Buddhism not only achieved new and astonishing
popularity within his domain but was carried beyond it by
missionaries among whom was probably at least one member of the emperor's immediate family.

It was during Asoka's reign, according to some, that the
Third Council of Buddhists was convened, and there is no
doubt that despite its vigor, or because of it, the Faith had

continued to produce sectarian divisions, and the lines of demarcation between the major groups of these had grown clearer.

Soon after Asoka's death the Maurya empire began to disintegrate, and a period of great political instability in northwest India resulted. There were invasions and the establishment of alien dynasties. It is now that the Hellenistic ruler Menandros, or Menander, appears, to be immortalized as the Milinda in the famous Buddhist treatise *Milinda Pañha* ("Questions of Milinda"). More important was a Kushan king named Kanishka who governed, as a result of conquest, a considerable empire stretching from the Aral Sea to some point beyond the Indus River. He may be regarded as, in a sense, the successor to Asoka in Buddhist lore because he too became the center of a cycle of legends and is said to have convened yet another great council of five hundred *Arhats* for the purpose of ascertaining the correct interpretation of Buddhist scripture. He commanded that the enormous commentaries which this scholarly group composed be engraved on copper sheets so that the true *dharma* might remain for posterity to enjoy. Alas, there are skeptics who, perhaps correctly, reject the story of this council and its prodigious labors. At any rate, the point of the Kanishka story is that as the Christian era approached, the concern for an orthodox understanding of Buddhism was reaching an intensity which proves the seriousness and breadth of the continuing doctrinal divisions. By this time it is possible to speak of the two powerful wings of Buddhism by the names which they bear to the present day: the Mahāyāna (self-styled "Great Way" or "Great Vehicle") which itself comprised a goodly number of sects, and their opponents whom they derisively named the Hīnayāna ("Lesser Vehicle") and who survive

to our times in the form of one sect, the Theravāda. Most
of the present book will be devoted to an analysis of the
main ideas of these two great factions as they survive to
the present.

We have seen that Buddhism broke into at least eighteen
"schools" at quite an early date, and that one of the common elements among them was a pluralistic analysis of
Reality which described as real an infinite series of marvelously brief and tiny "particles." Perhaps our best analogy for this concept may be drawn from a consideration of
time. If we ask what, in the flow of time, has "reality," we
confront an interesting problem. We can hardly say that
time *past* is real, for it survives only as memory; nor can
we say that the *future* is real, for it has not yet come. So
the "real" must be the present moment. But how shall we
catch a "present moment"? No sooner do we name it
"Now!" than it has fled. The real, then, seems to be a razor's
edge of time that can never be held, for its transience is
beyond imagination. Nor can we say that a moment, as it
dies, *causes* the next. It shapes the content of the next, but
it cannot cause it.

Here is a metaphor for the analysis of existence which
early Buddhist schools explored. To be sure, in addition to
the series of infinitely brief particles called *dharmas* (Pali:
dhammas, and often appropriately translated "point-instants"), all schools believed in at least one *dharma* which
was unconditioned by others and infinite in duration:
Nirvāna. But the universe was a continuous flow of rising
and dying *dharmas* with no stability or endurance to be
found in it, its ontological elements mutually conditioned
but each uncaused by the others.

By about the first century B.C., there arose, probably in

southern India, a movement calling itself the Mahāyāna.
Many of its ideas had been foreshadowed in earlier specu-
lations, but its final formulations represented a decisive
break with the older schools. To revert to our time imagery
again, if we do not wish to consider that the reality of
time is as fleeting as the *dharma* analysis suggests, we may
choose to consider time as a whole rather than as infinitely small segments of transient presentness. Thus there
is only *one* real entity—Time. The passing of moments is,
then, a phenomenon derived from what is real, but is
less than definitively real itself. Or, rather, Time is real;
the moment is neither real nor unreal in itself, but derives
a sort of reality from its status as the way in which Time
presents itself. This alternative more or less approximates
the concept of Reality advanced by the Mahāyāna schools
in their earliest phase.

The first of the great Mahāyāna schools called itself the
Mādhyamika, and its doctrines were systematized by a
genius named Nāgārjuna who may have lived during the
second century A.D. The second great Mahāyāna sect,
calling itself alternatively the Yogācāra or Vijñānavāda,
was allegedly founded by a shadowy figure named Maitreyanatha in about the third century A.D., but its most significant early philosophers were two brothers named Asanga
and Vasubandhu. Where the Mādhyamika had tried to
escape the dilemmas arising from either postulating the
solid reality of the material world or arguing for its
being mere appearance or "idea" (the alternatives represented in Western philosophy by realism and idealism),
the Yogācāra was strongly idealistic in tone, modifying
Mādhyamika's great concepts accordingly. Mahāyāna Buddhism has continued to contain both these facets, inter-

twined and sometimes in conflict ever since, and has
enjoyed a sectarian proliferation rivaling that of almost any
religious tradition.

The spirit of Mahāyāna was rather more liberal, doc-
trinally and in discipline, than that of Theravāda, and in
its hands, as we shall see, the earthly Buddha became
diminishingly important in relation to a cosmic Buddha-
Nature, omnipresent and unimaginable.

One must not suppose that Theravāda and Mahāyāna
have nothing in common. They share convictions about
the impermanence of all existent things, about the reality
of *karma*, of something we shall call transmigration; they
both adhere to the Buddha's twelvefold chain of conditioned co-production (a concept to be examined in Chapter V), to his description of the nature of life as inescapably
involved in suffering and ignorance, and to his promise
of *Nirvāna* as the end of Buddhist striving. But with all this
in common the divergence was enormous from the beginning and provoked the writing of much new material,
sometimes apologetic in nature, and (on the Mahāyāna
side) frequently taking the form of new scriptures, osten-
sibly bearing the authority of the Buddha.

The last great period of Buddhism in India coincided
with the Gupta era, founded by Chandragupta I, king of
Magadha, in 320 A.D. The rulers of this dynasty, although
not themselves Buddhists, were tolerant of the religion
and it was during their regime (in the early fifth century)
that the remarkable Buddhist university at Nālandā was
established.

With the decline of the Guptas we find Buddhism also
falling upon less lustrous days and by the seventh century the Chinese pilgrim Hsüan-tsang reports many ruined
temples and deserted monasteries, and serious outbreaks

of heresy. This decline continued and even gathered pace so that by the thirteenth century Buddhism was virtually extinct in its homeland.

One may speculate endlessly about the causes of the fatal illness of Buddhism within India, but some of the responsible factors are easy to specify. The popular character of Mahāyāna Buddhism tended to weaken the authority of the monastic elite, and the eventual arising of a Tantric version (a hybrid of Buddhism and ideas and practices common to Indian Tantrism in general) had further served to weaken institutionalized Buddhism by rendering it less easily distinguishable from other contemporary cults. Further, there was a surging movement of Hindu devotionalism within the cults associated with Vishnu and Śiva and these, like Tantrism, tended to absorb Buddhism (the Buddha himself was sometimes spoken of as an *avatar*, or incarnation of Vishnu). To the extent that they did not absorb Buddhism these devotional cults represented a powerful popular option. Finally we must reckon with Brahmin reaction, with occasional local persecutions, and with the assaults of Islam after the Muslim invasion of India. From the eighth century to the thirteenth century the Muslims wrought extensive havoc, destroying Buddhist buildings and dampening the ardor of devotees.

Thus Buddhism disappeared as an identifiable, independent entity; yet its influence continued to be felt and subsequent Indian philosophies, including those which repudiated Buddhism explicitly, assumed shapes that owed something to Buddhist ideas and criticism.

No less remarkable than Buddhism's decline in India was its flourishing elsewhere. Both Theravāda and Mahāyāna spread their arms to embrace vast areas and although they tended to receive local color wherever they went, they remained recognizable and reasonably faithful to their central affirmations. In Burma, Theravāda had to reach accommodation with the native animism, and learned at last to live side by side with it; in Tibet Mahāyāna had to assimilate the indigenous cults and wove a tapestry that at times shows patterns unguessed by the Buddha; but still Mahāyāna teachings can be recognized. Similarly in other lands Buddhism bent before a hundred winds, but never broke and never really ceased to assert itself in effective compromise.

For twenty centuries the teachings of the Buddha—or teachings said to be his—have nourished the hope and courage of millions throughout Asia. Theravāda established itself as the chief form of the Faith in Ceylon, Burma, Thailand, and Cambodia, and Mahāyāna dominated Bhutan, Nepal, Sikkim, Ladakh, Mongolia, Tibet, China, Korea, Vietnam, and Japan. In all these places the wisdom of Gautama has been held with varying degrees of understanding but always with veneration.

Thus Buddhism has endured as a persistent but most curious lotus. Refusing to remain rooted in its native pond, it has spread itself across the world. It is a vagrant lotus with no one place to call its home, for it thinks itself the Truth and it knows that truth is not at home in any one place but is the home of all.

Part Two
BUDDHIST PHILOSOPHY

III

BUDDHISM: RELIGION
OR PHILOSOPHY?

"Buddhism," according to Sir Monier Monier-Williams, "at least in its earliest and truest form, is no religion at all, but a mere system of morality and philosophy founded on a pessimistic theory of life."[1] Seldom has a notable scholar written a sentence so remarkably questionable from so many perspectives. In one respect, however, it is symptomatic of a recurrent Western bewilderment when confronted with Buddhism: it betrays a feeling that Buddhism, even if it performs a religious function for many people, lacks certain essential characteristics of a genuine religion. Just what those characteristics are depends rather heavily upon the presuppositions of individual analysts, but in the West they are inclined to be theistic: any structure of belief that does not include a necessary affirmation of God or of gods (or at least of some kind of supra-human entity worthy of worship) is not religious. However, the attempt to specify the essential elements of "religion" has met with so little agreement that judgments like Monier-Williams' remain uselessly arbitrary and mean little more than that Buddhism does not conform to his personal conception of religious phenomena.

Matters become more complicated because it is clear

that Buddhism (whether in theistic or non-theistic versions) does indeed serve a function which for some persons is served by Christianity, Islam, or Judaism—in short,
that it certainly has some functional qualities in common
with systems which most of us agree are religious. For this
reason Alfred North Whitehead tried to include Buddhism
in the field of religion, but still implied that its place there
was a little tenuous: Christianity, he said, "has always been
a religion seeking a metaphysic, in contrast to Buddhism
which is a metaphysic generating a religion." [2] Here we
find a suggestion that there is a difference between a religion and a metaphysic, but that each may have use of
the other. And now a Pandora's box has been opened, re-
leasing upon us an overpowering swarm of books and
articles dedicated to the exact analysis and definition of
"metaphysics," "religion," and "Buddhism."

The question that immediately arises is simple. What
does it matter whether we call Buddhism "religion" or
"metaphysics"? Call it what you will—invent a word if you
like—all that matters is Buddhism itself, not the convenient
category into which we consign it.

This cry of desperation is justified. We shall not bother
to spend much time comparing the merits of variant
definitions and categories, yet there is a certain minimal
discussion of religion and metaphysics (or philosophy)
that we must undertake if Buddhism itself is to be understood.

This book is concerned with Buddhism as philosophy,
which means that it will not discuss certain matters which
would be appropriate to a different perspective. It will not,
for instance, make much reference to the techniques of
meditation, the worship of celestial *bodhisattvas*, or the
recitation of sacred formulas. But one of the assumptions

which shall underlie all that follows is that Buddhist philosophy is only a part of a much broader phenomenon —a Buddhist religious tradition—and can be appreciated only when it is clearly seen as existing within the supportive and necessary framework of that entire system.

What, then, is a "religious tradition," and where does philosophy belong in such a context?

Men ask many questions about their existence. With more or less intensity we ask about the chemical constituents of our bodies, the bases of our patterns of behavior, the norms of human relationship, the origins and prospects of culture, and so on. But one of the most persistent enterprises of the human spirit is a questioning of the meaning and value of existence itself. Frequently a man feels that he has penetrated the mysteries of life and has found at least a clue to its meaning or meaninglessness. He may articulate this and share it, winning, at last, a following of admiring disciples. If he reaches the pinnacle of this process, the day comes when his ideas are taught in colleges and universities and every freshman can tell you exactly where he was wrong. He has become a philosopher.

But sometimes, rarely, the questioning of existence yields a different consequence. A man or a group of men profess to have discovered a truth so compelling and inclusive that it demands the total loyalty of our hearts and minds. It has been found not by a simple process of rationality alone, but by the bursting in upon men of an understanding for which our ordinary modes of thinking are not adequate. It is a truth that is somehow transcendent (beyond the range of our daily experience) yet which encloses us in a value or a purpose or a meaning that transforms us, makes us "whole," and fulfills perfectly the longing for meaning and completeness. The truth that has been immediately encountered may be called God or Void or Being or the Absolute or a hundred other names; it may be discussed in personal or impersonal terms, but it will certainly be felt to be a true foundation for adequate living and thinking. There will be a sense of having "leaped" to understanding; of having broken through (or having been delivered from) a bondage composed of commonsense, conventional logic, and "worldly" enslavement. Those who have had the experience of this truth feel liberated and immeasurably enriched.

Where the philosopher may have followers, the propounder of the sort of truth we are now discussing acquires devotees—if not to himself, then to the truth he presents. There is a measure of commitment beyond that which a philosophy can engender ("You shall love the Lord your God with all your heart, and with all your soul, and with all your might" [3]), and the object of this commitment is not an idea or a system of ideas but something which finally eludes adequate verbalization, so that even such words as "God" or "Truth" are not really proper designations for it.

In short, a religious tradition begins in an experience of transcendence. (Although that which is experienced may also be entirely immanent—within us—it is, however, transcendent of our usual ways of viewing ourselves or the world.) We may call this pristine sense of the Transcendent the "generating experience," for from it develops a tradition the chief goals of which are the enshrinement, description, expression, enjoyment, and perpetuation of the original experience itself.

The developing religious tradition becomes, or establishes, for its members a sort of subculture and this, in turn, interacting with the larger popular culture around it, modifies the latter and is modified until the two may finally become one unified entity. At this point we have a religious tradition which has also become a national or tribal "way of life," notable examples of which are to be found in the history of India, of medieval Europe, and of Islamic nations at least until the modern era. Thus there is probably a stage in the development of a great religion when it is a cultural aberration, an assault upon established values. If its attack is successful, those values are at last supplanted and the religion then becomes no longer the assailant, but the defender and endorser of the new social norms. In this process, however, it is doubtful whether a religion ever survives in its purity. It pays a price for its victory in the loss of some of the values and insights with which it began its career, and for this reason there will tend to be at least sporadic tensions within the religiously modified culture as the original but suppressed values try to reassert themselves. It may be that a religion has better prospects for retaining its original integrity if it never triumphs so completely that it becomes "established," but has instead to persist in constant interaction with a largely alien milieu.

In any event, a religious tradition aims at the recurrence of a generating experience of transcendent meaning or reality. It may eventually lose the will or the vision to perpetuate this aim, and if it does, it can no longer strictly be called "religious," for it has become a tradition without transcendence.

One of the more useful attempts to define "religion" is offered to us by Erich Fromm: Religion is "any system of thought and action shared by a group which gives the individual a frame of orientation and an object of devotion." [4] I would agree that religion is this, but not that everything conforming to this deserves to be called a religious tradition. I think that the experience of illumination, of seeing a truth or an "object of devotion" in some way beyond the ordinary world of perception is so important to the major religious systems that the concept of transcendence cannot be ignored.

Paul Tillich says that God is properly the legitimate object of man's ultimate concern and that to be religious —to have faith—is therefore to be in a state of ultimate concern.[5] This, too, is suggestive and useful. What I am contending here is that a religious *tradition* emerges only when an object of ultimate concern and of religious allegiance, however it may be symbolized, is believed to have been apprehended in a dynamic experience of intuitive immediacy, and when it is further believed that this experience can be cultivated or in some way repeated by and in the devotee. If one wishes to include, within the meaning of "religious" phenomena that do not conform to the description above, one is certainly entitled to do so. But there are systems of commitment that do conform to it, and these are so significant in the history of mankind that they deserve special classification. For the purposes of this study the term "religious tradition" will be reserved for structures the character of which fits the outline we have drawn.

The object of religious allegiance need not be a theistic image of God, but it must be more than an abstract concept or ideational system. From the apprehension of it philosophy and ethics will flow, but the immediacy of encounter with it is always the essential fact to which a religious tradition points, usually as its origin and always as its goal. This is why Martin Luther was essentially correct in insisting that "faith" dominate "works" in Christian thinking, for if action becomes an end in itself we have a "mere" system of ethics. Works must serve faith, and faith must be understood not as blind acceptance of curious ideas, but rather as a direct relationship to God, before action (or "works") can be part of an authentically *religious* tradition. And this is why some men who bravely discuss the meaning of life are philosophers whereas others become founders of great religions; but perhaps a concrete illustration of the difference between religious and purely philosophical figures will help.

One of the foremost of modern mathematicians was the late Norbert Wiener. Being a man of sensitivity and intelligence, Wiener expended some of his analytical skill upon life itself as well as upon his chosen scholarly field, and he produced a beautifully succinct and lucid statement of his conclusions:

> We are swimming upstream against a great torrent of disorganization, which tends to reduce everything to the heat-death of equilibrium and sameness described in the second law of thermodynamics. . . . In this, our main obligation is to establish arbitrary enclaves of order and system. These enclaves will not remain there indefinitely by any momentum of their own after we have once established them. Like the Red Queen, we cannot stay where we are without running as fast as we can.
>
> We are not fighting for a definitive victory in the indefinite future. It is the greatest possible victory to be, to continue to be, and to have been. No defeat can deprive us of the success of having existed for some moment of time in a universe that seems indifferent to us.[6]

We find here a statement about what we may profitably do with our lives and about whatever value and meaning life may assume in the presence of the ambiguities of suffering, frustration, encroaching disorder, and death.

Here is at least a seed of a possible philosophical system.

Compare with this Gautama's famous Four Noble Truths. We have already met these, so we shall be content with a bald paraphrase of them here. He taught that (1) to exist is to suffer; (2) the cause of suffering is ignorant craving; (3) ignorant craving can be overcome; (4) the way to defeat craving is to follow the Eightfold Path of discipline. Here, as in Weiner's statement, we find a suggestion that there is something we may usefully do with a life in which the fact of suffering in its various forms cannot be avoided. But Gautama's teaching is part of a great religious tradition; Weiner's is a private reflection with, no doubt, a few assentors. Even if Weiner's comments came to be universally believed, and a world culture was framed around them, however, they would not establish a religious tradition *until and unless* there was added to them the belief that Weiner was expressing a truth discovered in a moment of illumination in which he felt himself transcending the methods and resources of normal reflection; a truth available to others in a similar illuminative experience. It is precisely the fact that Gautama's teaching came to be associated with such a moment of transcendental awareness, and that the release from suffering which he offered came to be seen as entailing the repetition of at least something approximating that awareness, that allowed Gautama to become no mere philosopher but the founder of a religion. What Gautama "saw" was no set of sentences, but an Absolute Truth which the propositions he began to proclaim merely heralded. What he saw was *Nirvāna*—that which is at once the Truth and the ultimately important Reality, and it transcended anything that could be apprehended by ordinary logic or empiricism.

Religion, then, begins, or at least is believed by its adherents to begin, in an experience of transcendence. We must make it clear, however, that the experience which initiates a religion and which is thereafter sought by the devotees need not be that of the acknowledged founder. In Christianity, for example, it is not the religious experience of Jesus that is sought by the orthodox, for he is believed to be unique. Rather, men feel today the desire to experience *him* and God as manifested through him in the way they were known by the first Christians. It is the apostles who should be regarded as the true founders of Christianity and whose awakening experience is to be recaptured by us, whereas Jesus is unique as the concretely enfleshed Word and Act of the Supreme Reality who is the Object of devotion and the Truth to be encountered.

Now we are at the point of understanding the place of a religious metaphysic within the larger religious tradition, but before we proceed to that we must face a couple of possible objections to what has so far been said.

Like any generalization about religion, the theory of a central generating experience is surely at best unprovable and at worst considerably shaken by the data of primitive cultures. Are there not many peoples whose religious traditions fail to disclose the memory of a great foundational moment in which some person or group experienced the Transcendent?

In the first place we must point out that our objective in this chapter is not to establish a general law which shall govern the origin of all religions, but merely to outline a process of development sufficiently common to be useful as a guide in studying the relations of the various elements within a major, sophisticated religious tradition. But, in

addition, it seems entirely possible that one could defend
the idea that the religious element of every primitive culture—insofar as it is truly "religious" and not magical—
can be shown to point to the possibility of an encounter
with supramundane reality, and that this possibility will
be felt to exist either for all men or at least for enough
representative men that the community can be served. If
this is true, I suspect that such a belief will have arisen
in some generative or foundation moment, even if this is
undemonstrable now because it is so far forgotten as not
to appear even in disguised form in a myth.

In other words, I think that the authentically religious
facets of primitive cultures tend to support, or at least not
to refute, the theory outlined above, but even if there are
exceptional religious cultures, the function of this theory
remains intact so long as it serves as a useful tool for
studying the inner relations of religions to which it does
apply.

Another objection may be raised: if the theory fails to
serve a *major* religiocultural system, surely its usefulness
is greatly diminished as an analytical guide, and just as
surely it will have difficulty applying to Hinduism. Where
can we find evidence for the generative experience in this
religious heritage, so rich, so influential, but so vague in
origin?

Again we must respond that the theory's usefulness
depends upon its effectiveness as a working tool, not upon
our capacity to document its exact historical accuracy. The
Vedas and especially the Upanishads themselves enshrine
the pristine religious experience upon which modern
Hinduism is built, and there can be no doubt that Indian
thought is rich in the suggestion that the goal of religious
endeavor is more than ethics (in which, indeed, it tends

to be rather weak) or even philosophy. That we cannot name a man or a group of men who were the first in any particular tradition to "know" the experience from which the tradition issues does not much matter. The hypothesis of such an experience explains facets of the distinctively religious phenomenon with illuminative power.

How, then, does the generative experience yield at last the fruit of a broad religious tradition?

After the initial discovery of the Transcendent there is an attempt to relate what has been experienced to the general environment. What it means for and in a particular culture, a natural order of mountains, rivers, trees, a social milieu of friends and enemies, wise men and fools—all this must be considered in order that he who has known the Transcendent may still feel unified and not torn between two worlds. Out of this engagement of the generating experience and the environment there gradually emerges a cumulative tradition exploring, expounding, and expressing the experience and its meaning in the environment. This tradition, as we have said, becomes the vehicle upon which the generating experience attempts to move across time and space, and it invariably contains a number of facets, some of the most important of which are illustrated in the diagram at the top of page 60.

Many of the elements listed in the diagram are so obviously part of religious traditions that little need be said about them, but a brief explanation is doubtless in order.

It is almost instinctive in man to think about his most remarkable or valued experiences, so it is inevitable that a religion shall gather within its cumulative tradition some speculation in the form of philosophy or theology (the distinction between these two forms of reflection is elusive

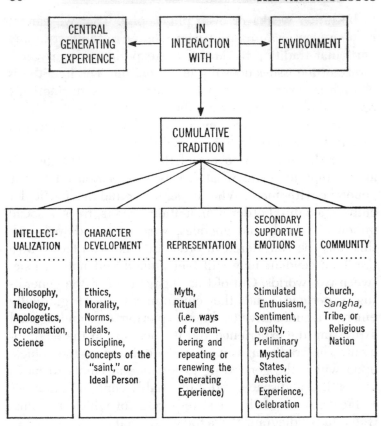

but need not occupy us now). When a religion must make
its way in a culture that contains alternative structures of
value, it is just as inevitable that it shall develop a body of
thought designed to recommend or defend it, thus apol-
ogetics sooner or later appear together with more or less
conventional forms of proclamation. Among the proclama-
tory forms will be drama and art as well as stereotyped
argument, but all will be designed to set forth a reasonable and attractive presentation of the dominant religious

convictions. Science belongs to the intellectual parapher-
nalia of religion when persons within the tradition use the
methods or data of science to examine their own religious
phenomena (for instance, a sympathetic study of the so-
ciology of religion, the psychology of religion, and so on)
or when they engage in a general scientific enterprise on
the basis of premises drawn from the tradition, and thus
attempt to show that the world can be understood most
fully from a point of view which arises within their religious framework (the work of Teilhard de Chardin often
falls into this category). Thus religious intellectualization
takes a number of forms, but all of them remain wedded
to the cumulative tradition and its central generative experience.

Similarly, a religion usually tends to develop expecta-
tions about behavior on the part of its members, together
with an image of the sort of character that is the ideal
outcome of religious commitment, as well as methods of
discipline, moral values, and even an ethical system or
systems to promote the desired result. Here is another
facet of the burgeoning tradition.

Further, a community develops among those who have
had or who wish to have the religious experience and who
share, as a consequence, certain beliefs and attitudes, and
this community soon becomes institutionalized, falling
into patterns of organization which often endure long
after they have ceased effectively to serve their constituents. Communities and their structural norms comprise
yet another element in the emerging tradition, and where
the religion fails to become so unanimously accepted that
it is integrally merged with the general culture, these community structures are often instrumental in defining de-
fensively the uniqueness of the religious people and in

providing them with a sense of belonging which supports their faith. Outstanding examples in the United States are Amish or Mennonite communities, but denominations and sects are less striking instances of the same phenomenon. The tradition gathers a group of people who belong to it and must order their common life accordingly. Eventually the community begins to include members with little interest in the experience of transcendence but with a desire to be associated with some other feature of the cumulative tradition—perhaps its ethics, theology, or sense of identity.

When we come to a consideration of what I have called "secondary supportive emotions" we enter a realm of extreme complexity which has yet to receive its first adequate exploration. William James's *Varieties of Religious Experience* is deservedly a classic, but it is no more than a gentle (and today rather archaic) breeze disturbing the surface of a very deep sea. Subsequent studies in the psychology of religion are often valuable footnotes, but this field is a mine (to change our metaphor) whose riches are strangely elusive. Within this category we find a range of "feeling" responses which are somehow regarded as appropriate to various objects of value within the tradition and even to the Transcendent Object itself. We have, for instance, the carefully stimulated enthusiasm of a frontier revival meeting in Protestant Christianity, the subtly cultivated aesthetic mood of a tea ceremony in a Zen temple, the preliminary trance states with their almost satisfying peace which a Buddhist traditionally learns to cultivate on his way to *Nirvāna*, the feeling of solitary and meritorious submission of a displaced Afghan camel driver as he prays to Allah in the Australian desert, and an almost infinite variety of other emotions all of which support the faith of the participant and sustain him in his quest for the ultimate attainment that his religion offers. The celebration of whatever a religion proclaims as the triumph it offers, whether salvation, enlightenment, or life, is perhaps the supreme among these supportive emotions, but all of them are important and may actually become substitute satisfactions for the transcendence experience itself, especially when confidence in attaining this is lost or, as is often the case, when it is not seriously desired because of its potential for the disruption of a comfortable value system in which it serves as a nominal ideal.

Finally, an item of every great religious tradition is representation: the re-presentation of its basic data in myth and ritual. The purpose of this performance is to remember the event which justifies the continuing cultus and, beyond this, to re-create it if possible—that is, to establish the conditions in which others may now find repeated within themselves the central generating experience of the tradition.

A religious tradition, then, presents a spectrum of related phenomena and the study of any of these in isolation will inevitably lose sight of some of the tradition's significance. We are about to examine some of the ideas of Buddhism—some of its philosophy—but we need to remember that Buddhism is more than philosophy and would not endure as the primary allegiance of so many people if it were not. Most Buddhists, indeed, have a very poor understanding of Buddhist philosophy; most have read little, if any, of the scripture of their religion. For the fact is that an individual never makes use of all the resources of the tradition to which he belongs. In fact, he probably never entirely apprehends the whole of any one element, but he certainly emphasizes some to the exclusion of others. A Christian, for instance, may be strongly committed to what he holds to be the ethical norm of his faith yet know very little theology, be largely indifferent to the church, suspicious of all religious emotion, and rarely a participant in Christian ritual. Whether such a person would be recognizable as a Christian to St. Paul is another question (which we may conveniently leave to St. Paul), but he is a member of a traditional religious community in some measure, even though he makes use of only a fragment of its richness. Similarly Buddhists need not indulge in much philosophical speculation to be Buddhists. Buddhist philosophy exists as a subordinate part of something very much broader. Remembering that, we shall not assume we "know" Buddhism if someday we find ourselves reasonably acquainted with its metaphysics.

IV

THE NATURE OF REALITY AND THE GROUND OF VALUE

THERĀVADA

The basic teachings of Theravāda Buddhism are contained in the so-called *Tipiṭaka,* or "Three Baskets."[1] These collections of scripture consist of the *Vinaya Piṭaka* ("discipline basket") in which rules for the living of a Buddhist life, especially by a monk, are carefully set out; the *Sutta Piṭaka* ("sermon basket"), which contains the more general teaching of the Buddha; and the *Abhidhamma Piṭaka* ("exposition basket") in which the themes raised in the *suttas* are expanded to suit the tastes and needs of Buddhist philosophers who could not rest entirely content with the more simple, and sometimes more ambiguous, teachings left by the Master. Many of the ideas with which we shall be dealing in this and subsequent chapters are, therefore, found in their simplest extant form in the *Sutta Piṭaka,* but our understanding of them depends upon their development in the later *abhidhamma* literature.

At this point we must interpose a note about spelling. The scriptural language of Theravāda is Pali, whereas that of early Mahāyāna Buddhism is Sanskrit. These are closely related tongues, and even in transliteration the connection between them is usually obvious. To avoid confusion, however, from this point on we shall consistently use the Sanskrit form of whatever technical words from these languages we incorporate into the text, but when we are discussing Theravāda we shall, at the first use of such a word, add the Pali version in parentheses.

Gautama (Gotama) the Buddha did not teach in a philosophical vacuum, and much of what he had to say was addressed, in reaction, to prevailing schools of thought. Against hedonists he taught that even pleasure is finally unsatisfactory because it passes; against mystics he taught that their mystical trances and attendant peace, although offering great solace, were "mind-produced" and had little to do with truth.[2] But two of his favorite targets were at opposite ends of a philosophical arc: eternalists and nihilists. In refuting these, he incidentally abandoned the massively influential idealistic monism of much Indian thought.

In beginning his own quest for truth, Gautama had used as his fixed reference point the fact that there is suffering inescapably involved in life, and this suffering is largely compounded of frustration and disappointment. It is not the case that life has no pleasures, but that its pleasures do not provide final and unending satisfaction. But why does the passing of the pleasant and good bring pain? Here emerged a fundamental, but very simple, insight: there is in us a persistent longing to endure and to enjoy, and our suffering arises largely because nothing in us can forever do the latter and nothing around us the former. The fundamental and most ubiquitous fact of existence is flux: not that some *thing* is constantly undergoing change while remaining in some secluded essence identical with all its emerging forms, but rather that there is no permanence whatever. There is change but no thing that changes while remaining in some sense the same thing throughout. Within existence there is absolutely nothing that comes to be which does not utterly fail to be at some subsequent time. Our suffering, then, arises because we hope for permanence where there can be none, and this error arises because of our ignorance about the truth of existence and our foolish craving to be and to have what cannot exist within the realm of all that comes into being.

It was not new in India to argue that there was no lasting objective entity, but the question of whether there was an immortal Subject was another matter. It might be that everything I see is not only transitory but actually quite unreal (except as a product of imagination), yet surely the "I" that sees or imagines is real and substantial enough. Surely there is within me, a "self" that acts, perceives, and suffers, remaining the same self through all the changes that age and circumstance bring to me. Gautama seems to have believed that conventional Indian thought about the *Ātman* (*Attā*)—the divine, immortal element in man—was affirming precisely such an eternal individuality for each of us. That he was mistaken in this assumption has been pointed out many times and is of little consequence to us at present. What does matter is that in announcing his famous "no *Ātman*" doctrine he was staunchly denying that any permanence can be found either in our subjectivity or in what it perceives.

Gautama himself was evidently more concerned with showing that there is no permanent self than with demonstrating that external, objective reality is also transient. This is probably the case because his original quest was for the defeat of suffering and he found that if men

stopped trusting in or hoping for personal endurance, they
had overcome the single most compelling illusion imprison-
ing them. Further, if (as he believed) Brahmin as well as
Jain philosophers were really saying that there is in us a
perfect, changeless "soul," or essence, and if it is further
true, as Gautama's observations assured him, that we are
in a state of illusion and affliction, it follows that there is
no hope for an improvement in our condition. What is
changeless and eternal cannot become better than it is
and cannot even cease to be. To be desperately unsatisfied
with one's state and to be eternally unchanging did not
seem to Gautama an enviable situation, and the conviction
that *nothing* is eternal or without change seemed to him
a much more comforting matter. The idea that constant
change is the character of all sentience ensures the possibility of improvement in our lot.

But there are problems in the idea that nothing in me
endures. Gautama meant that my life is a series of moments and that nothing in me remains the same from one
of those moments to the next. Yet I remember so much.
And my friends, whom I have not seen since yesterday,
recognize me and use a name that I recognize as "mine."
Surely there is something that persists. Surely there is
some sense in which I am the same person who was born
those many years ago.

Gautama's response to such an argument presents unnecessary difficulties to us today unless we recognize that
he had certain presuppositions about the meaning of such
ideas as "self," or "ego," and "soul" which we do not
ordinarily take for granted. He identified the self that men
claimed to be or to have with the *Ātman* of earlier Indian
speculation, and because this was always regarded as
autonomous, permanent, blissful, and perfect, he denied

its existence. Nothing empirical has this combination of qualities.

Further, whereas modern thinkers tend to regard the ego, or self, as a function, Gautama assumed that it must (if it existed at all) have substance, and therefore when we have sifted out all its accidents, it should remain in its purity for us to see. But when all human elements are analyzed, there is no perceivable underlying entity that can be isolated as the bearer of the functions of personhood. We know what it means to "see" and we know what an eye is, but can we ever see what sees by means of the eye? The function and organ of seeing exist, then, but why argue for a seer who transcends both function and organ? We know what it means to exist, and we perceive in a human being many existent parts and qualities, but why argue for the reality of something to bear those parts and qualities? The most famous exposition of this point comes from a noncanonical work called "Questions of Milinda" in which a king named Milinda is questioning a Buddhist sage, Nāgasena. Since the passage of relevance is both lucid and important, I shall quote it at length.

Nāgasena, in response to the king's request, tells him his name, but then remarks that there is, of course, no real individual signified by the name, no actual self. The king thinks that this is absurd and asks Nāgasena to justify the strange assertion. The monk responds:

"Tell me, did you come on foot or in a vehicle?"

"Reverend Sir, I do not travel on foot; I came in a chariot."

"If, great king, you came in a chariot, tell me about the chariot. Pray, great king, is the pole the 'chariot'?"

"No indeed, Reverend Sir."

"Is the axle the 'chariot'?"

"No indeed, Reverend Sir."

"Are the wheels the 'chariot'?"

"No indeed, Reverend Sir."

"Is the chariot-body the 'chariot'?"

"No indeed, Reverend Sir."

"Is the flagstaff of the chariot the 'chariot'?"

"No indeed, Reverend Sir."

"Is the yoke the 'chariot'?"

"No indeed, Reverend Sir."

"Are the reins the 'chariot'?"

"No indeed, Reverend Sir."

"Is the goad-stick the 'chariot'?"

"No indeed, Reverend Sir."

"Well, great king! Is the sum total of pole, axle, wheels, chariot-body, flagstaff, yoke, reins, and goad—is this the 'chariot'?"

"No indeed, Reverend Sir."

"Well, great king! Is something other than the sum total of pole, axle, wheels, chariot-body, flagstaff, yoke, reins, and goad—is this the 'chariot'?"

"No indeed, Reverend Sir."

"Great king, I have asked you every question I can think of, but I cannot discover the 'chariot'! Apparently the 'chariot' is nothing but a sound! But, great king, what is there about all this that is the 'chariot'? Great king, you utter untruth, you utter falsehood, when you say: 'There is no "chariot."'"

To all this the king, rather on the defensive, replies:

"Reverend Nāgasena, I do not utter falsehood. Because of the pole, and because of the axle, and because of the wheels, and because of the chariot-body, and because of the flagstaff, the epithet, designation, appellation, style, name—'chariot'—comes into use."

This is the moment to which Nāgasena has carefully built, and he hastens to make his point:

"Great king, you understand perfectly what a chariot is.

And precisely the same thing is true with reference to me also. Because of the hair of the head, and because of the hair of the body, and because of the nails, and because of the teeth, and because of the skin, and because of the flesh, and because of the sinews, and because of the bones, and because of the marrow of the bones, and because of the kidneys, and because of the heart, and because of the liver, and because of the peritoneum, and because of the spleen, and because of the lungs, and because of the intestines, and because of the mesentery, and because of the stomach, and because of the faeces, and because of the bile, and because of the phlegm, and because of the pus, and because of the blood, and because of the sweat, and because of the fat, and because of the tears, and because of the serum, and because of the saliva, and because of the mucus of the nose, and because of the grey matter in the skull, and because of Form, and because of Sensation, and because of Perception, and because of the States of Mind, and because of Consciousness—because of all these there comes into use the epithet, designation, appellation, style, name—but name only—'Nāgasena.' In the highest sense of the word, however, no 'individual' is thereby assumed to exist." [3]

The point of this argument is, of course, that a man is a composite of many physical and psychological elements, but that there is no unifying "entity," or self, which owns these things—there is literally nothing but a combination of parts and activities. If a man were to dismantle a car hoping to find, somewhere in there, an essence of "carness," he would be disappointed. Similarly, if you take a man apart in order to uncover *his* essence or soul or selfhood, you will find nothing. A man *is* his physical and psychological parts and functions—nothing more. There is, thus, no immortal center in a man, and all that the word "man" names is transient. *Becoming*, not *Being*, is the character of existence.

Having gone so far, the Buddha—or someone soon after him—began to analyze our existence into five components called *skandhas* (*khandhas*) in order to show more clearly the insubstantiality of our being and experience, and to help to dispel the illusion that we may hope for immortality in ourselves or in something else. It is to this analysis we must next turn.

Skandhas

The Pali *sūtras* (*suttas*)—scriptures purporting to be the sermonic teaching of the Buddha—are generally content to remain with the fivefold division of reality that follows here, and only in the *abhidharma* (*abhidhamma*) do we find much further development. It is probable, therefore, that the *skandhas* represent an analysis sufficiently profound for the purposes of early Buddhism and for the essential message of Buddhist preaching.

Our human existence is composed of elements that may themselves be classified as comprising five "heaps" or aggregates or sets called *skandhas*. Each *skandha* must be understood to be not a thing but a group, and they are as follows:

rūpa (*rūpa*): literally, "form" or "shape." This refers roughly to the object of our concept of matter and, in a human being, it consists of the body and everything that is to be found in us except moral and mental qualities. It includes, for instance, our sense organs and also the objects they apprehend.

vedanā (*vedanā*): This is sometimes translated "sen-

sation," but it is closer to what we usually mean by
"feeling." Its contents are further divided into pleasant,
unpleasant, and neutral, and it is often related to sensation in such a way that its most common use clearly
refers to feelings stimulated by sensory impressions.

samjña (*sañña*): These are perceptions which are the
result of the function of sense organs including *manas*
(*mano*), the sixth sense organ in Buddhist psychology;
a mental function of judgment, calculation, and synthesis that produces ideas.

saṃskāra (*sankhāra*): Probably best translated "coef-
ficients," although "tendencies," "confections," and
other terms have been suggested. This includes impulses, predispositions, volitions, emotions, habits, and
all the mental concomitants of consciousness as the Buddhist understands this.

vijñāna (*viññāna*): "Awareness," or "consciousness."
This should not be confused with *saṃskāra* which includes the functions or attendants of consciousness.
Obviously until *vijñāna* comes into existence *saṃskāra*
cannot do so, and, rather less obviously, neither can any
of the others according to conventional Theravādin
philosophy.

Here, then, are all the components of our existence and
once we have assigned to each its proper role, there remains nothing for the illusory ego, or self, to do. One may
argue that *vijñāna*, consciousness, presupposes a subject
who is conscious, but Gautama taught that although sense
experience is dependent upon *vijñāna*, it is also true that
vijñāna rests upon the work of each of the senses and
needs only them to perform its function.[4]
Indeed one may—and Buddhists did—divide *vijñāna*

into six subcategories, one for each of the senses including
manas. There is, thus, eye consciousness, ear consciousness,
and so on, and without the momentary element of consciousness there can be no seeing; yet the consciousness
that contains awareness *of* something seen is equally dependent upon the organ and operation of sight. Consciousness of something, then, is the product of one or more of
the senses and *vijñāna* and not of any underlying entity
that possesses these but is itself inscrutable.

The first expansion of this simple analysis consisted of
the elaboration of the experiences of consciousness into
categories called in Pali *āyatanas* and *dhātus*. The consequent system may be the result of a very naïve psychology, but it is also a pleasant example of the Indian fondness for multiplying categories and I suspect that, far from
originating it, the Buddha himself would have found the
entire structure largely irrelevant. We should, however, at
least have the outline of this system before us as we
proceed to the rather more ingenious developments yet to
come.[5]

Āyatanas

The meaning of *āyatana* is essentially "ground" or "field"
of consciousness, and the *āyatanas* were twelve in number, consisting of the sense organs and their respective
fields of perception:

1. the organ of sight   2. the object of sight
3. the organ of hearing   4. the object of hearing
5. the organ of smell   6. the object of smell
7. the organ of taste   8. the object of taste
9. the organ of touch   10. the object of touch
11. the organ of thought   12. the object of thought

The purpose of this analysis was largely functional: the Buddhist, meditating on this division of consciousness into twelve related factors, should at last find no need to postulate or believe in that troublesome and unreal additional entity, the self. Consciousness is entirely accounted for by the interaction of these twelve *āyatanas* and it is philosophically uneconomical and unnecessary to add anything more.

We have already said a word about *manas*, the organ of thought that is the sixth sense organ in many Indian systems of psychology, but a further explanatory note may now be useful. In a sense *manas* is the root of our basic trouble as human beings, for it is the manufacturer of the illusion of individual selfhood, but it is also the organ by means of which we turn from error and begin the difficult path to freedom. It is the organ of intellection and it has certain clearly defined operations to perform:

1. It receives and organizes the raw data provided by the five other senses. That is, when the eye provides redness and roundness, the nose offers the sweet smell of ripe apple, the fingers sense smooth firmness, and so on, the *manas* puts all these impressions together and constructs the concept "apple." The other senses perceive, but *manas* conceives—it transforms naked perceptions into meaningful thought objects.

2. *Manas* is also that organ which provides judgment, foresight, memory, imagination, and rational reflection. Closely related to this is a third function.

3. *Manas* gives birth to the sense of "I" and "mine"; it distinguishes between that which I am and that which is not myself. When a baby first meets a resistance (the sides of his crib, a recalcitrant mother) and discovers that there is something that is not himself—and therefore, by in-

ference, that there is something that *is* himself—*manas* is
at work, spinning the data of the other senses into a concept of exclusivity and selfhood.

4. *Manas* provides volition, and since only willed and
conscious acts produce karmic consequences (a fact that
we shall discuss at greater length later), it is *manas* that
provokes the structure of cause and effect in which we find
ourselves imprisoned and suffering. But it is also *manas*
that begins to will the discipline of the Eightfold Path by
which we shall at last break out of our illusion and bondage.

So far, then, we have organs and objects of consciousness forming a twelvefold process of subjectivity without
a personal, individual subject. One further development
in this line of analysis was yet forthcoming: the *dhātus*.

Dhātus

Dhātu means "element" and our subjective experience
was divided, at last, into eighteen of these. Actually, however, we find here only the now familiar *āyatanas* plus the
actual states of consciousness that they produce. The list,
which certainly needs no explanation, is as follows:

1. Organ of sight,
2. Object of sight,
3. State of consciousness resulting from the experience of seeing.

4. Organ of hearing,
5. Object of hearing,
6. State of consciousness resulting from the experience of hearing.

7. Organ of smell,
8. Object of smell,
9. State of consciousness resulting from the experience of smelling.

10. Organ of taste,
11. Object of taste,
12. State of consciousness resulting from the experience of tasting.

13. Organ of touch,
14. Object of touch,
15. State of consciousness resulting from the experience of touching.

16. Organ of mentation,
17. Object of mentation,
18. State of consciousness resulting from the experience of mentation.

Here was an attempt to analyze the factors of existence on the basis of human subjectivity; it is essentially a psychlogical analysis, and a remarkably simple one. Its problems, indeed, are most conspicuously that it is too subjective and too simple to satisfy the philosophical intelligence, and it could not have been long before a rather different and more objective analysis began to be attempted. The *abhidharma* material is very largely devoted to this new analysis and we must content ourselves with a bare introduction, specifying only the more important elements in it and merely suggesting the complexity that developed.

Dharmas

In introducing the elaborate *abhidharma* analysis of existence, we must first guard against possible confusion by briefly discussing the various meanings of the word *dharma* (*dhamma*), since this is the most important single term with which we shall be dealing. It is doubtful whether any word has had a more colorful or complex career in Indian philosophy, and its meanings are so curiously diverse that some outline of them should probably appear early in every discussion of either Hindu or Buddhist thought. Of its meanings the most common and important are these:

1. Tradition or teaching. Thus one may speak of the Buddha's entire system of ideas as his *dharma*.
2. Duty. In India, to be a member of a particular caste has historically meant to have certain inescapable obligations—a *dharma*—the performance of which is righteousness, the non-performance unrighteousness.
3. Natural law. The order of the universe is its *dharma*.
4. Objects of perception: the data, at least believed to be authentic, of experience and observation.
5. A basic element of existence.
6. The one inclusive Reality: the Absolute.

In the present discussion it is with the fifth meaning that we are concerned, although all the others have important places in Buddhist discussion.

The *dhātus* had been an attempt to press beyond the *skandha* analysis in order to disclose even more clearly the

insubstantial nature of things, but they had been understood in terms of consciousness. It is true that in addition
to organs of perception and the experience of consciousness there had been mention of objects of awareness, showing that no reversion to a typical Indian idealism was intended, but *dhātus* were still rooted in a subjectivist perspective. With the idea of *dharmas* the focus shifted. Now
the realm of objective reality is given more emphasis and
it is to be understood that we are dealing with real entities
which underlie or comprise the *skandhas* themselves.

Dharmas are the ultimate elements in existence. They
are impersonal, simple entities, the fundamental building
blocks of all that we are or know. In some respects they
are like the atoms of Democritus, except that they are
more elusive, having as nearly as possible no extension in
space or duration in time. They have, as a consequence,
often been described as "point-instants." On the subject of
duration there was some argument among early Buddhist
schools, but Theravādins generally maintained that a
purely subjective *dharma* (a "thought *dharma*") had a
life-span of "three moments" (the moments of birth,
maturity, and demolition), whereas material *dharmas*
survived through four moments (birth, maturity, decay,
and decease). The crucial fact is, however, that these
"moments" cannot be related to any measurable period of
time and the discussion is really concerned not with duration but with stages of evolution.

Dharma analysis served admirably the goal of emphasiz-
ing the transience of things. Everything we see is not really
a thing at all but a collection of *dharmas,* and every
dharma in the collection is a point-instant. The change
that occurs in things is far more rapid and complete than
our ordinary perception leads us to imagine, for it is not

the case that anything remains constant. Change is the
replacement of one *dharma* by another, the former having
utterly ceased to be, and the latter ceasing to be almost
as soon as it arises.

One can, for convenience, talk about *skandhas, āyatanas,
dhātus*, and so on, but what must above all be understood
is that only the *dharmas*—these final, elementary particles
—are real in themselves, anything else being merely a
compound of them.

One can imagine the impact of such thinking when it
was first introduced into India. First, it must have offended
the eternalists, because everything was so extraordinarily
transient. Second, it wounded the nihilists because
dharmas were actually *there* and kept arising in an apparently eternal process. Third, the idealists and the mon-
ists were offended because this was obviously a theory of
radical realistic pluralism. Existence, at any given moment, consisted not of *one* entity but of many.

There are two chief classes of *dharma:* the conditioned
and the unconditioned. All the *dharmas* of ordinary, phenomenal existence are conditioned, bound in a chain of
dependence upon other *dharmas* or upon the four natural
elements (whose place in all this is rather ambiguous),
but there was some argument among the schools about the
number of unconditioned, completely autonomous *dharmas*. For some, there was only one—*Nirvāna* (*Nibbāna*)—
but for others space was also unconditioned, and occasion-
ally there were several items in this category. *Nirvāna*
was certainly the chief and most authoritative claimant to
the honor.

The four "natural elements"—earth, air, fire, and water
—are not integrated into this *dharma* scheme with convincing clarity at any stage, but it is taught that every

unit of perceptible matter actually contains all four, although one will inevitably so dominate that it alone is detected by our senses. The elements, however, are often allowed to fade into oblivion as actual "stuff" and to survive chiefly as functions. Thus, earth has the function of supporting existents, water's task is providing cohesion—holding things together, fire is a ripening agent, and air is an expanding one. This description of the elements and their functions, however, has something of the character of a footnote and is peripheral to the essential *dharma* analysis.

In time the *dharmas* were made the component particles not only of material reality but of mental life as well, and impressive lists were prepared (differing from school to school) categorizing mental properties and thus attempting to spell out in detail the *dharma* structure of thought. There were classes of "Universal Mental Properties" consisting of *dharmas* common to every act of thought, "Particular Mental Properties" which are restricted to certain specific types of thought, and the further division of all these into meritorious, demeritorious, and neutral. To pursue this theme would take us far beyond the scope of an introductory book, and those who wish to explore a little further should now resort to McGovern's *Manual of Buddhist Philosophy* or to Conze's *Buddhist Thought in India.*

The essential point to glean from all that has been said so far is that Theravāda Buddhism set out to demolish any pretensions the mortal human being may have, or may think he has, to inherent immortality. In this it is as radical as Judaism or early Christianity and is far more concerned than they to propose an ontological theory that supported and tried to explain its conviction of universal transience. Of the problems that arose in conjunction with the development of this system the most important, and enduring, has been that of accounting for experienced continuity and identity. If reality is, at base, a continuum of discrete entities, what binds them into recognizable patterns? Nāgārjuna, the great Mahāyānist, may have had his Theravādin rivals in mind when he said that those who deny "Emptiness"—the Mahāyāna concept of the Absolute —but continue to believe in existence are "like a horseman who forgets that he is on horseback." [6] Is a stream of exceedingly transient entities a sufficient explanation of phenomena, or should we, like Thomas Aquinas, feel that even an eternal chain of dependent events is not self-explanatory? These are questions for our own reflection, and we must press on now to another part of Theravādin philosophy.

Cosmology

Like other sections of Buddhist philosophy, cosmology is an intricate and colorful garden, full of variety.[7] There has, of course, been development through the ages, and Mahāyāna has its own flavor, but the central ideas remain fairly consistent to the present day. It seems probable that the next few decades will see a considerable revision of much Buddhist cosmology, and in any case most of it is not essential to the dominant center of the tradition, so we will confine ourselves to a mere outline.

There are several ways of thinking about the universe in Buddhism, and they are not, at all points, easy to integrate. Like most Indian philosophies, Buddhism thought that the universe contained an infinite number of worlds and that each was, in major details at least, identical with our own. Each had similar geographical features and was attended by a similar structure of heavens and hells. Each world may, thus, be thought of as a series of "levels" with Mount Meru marking the center. Next to *Nirvāna* itself the level of human existence is, in many respects, the most fortunate of all, for it is here alone that striving to attain *Nirvāna* is possible. Below, in the levels of suffering, one is entirely preoccupied with one's misery, and in the heavens above our level there is too much delight or peace to encourage the seeking of ultimate release. Man, however, enjoys a blend of suffering and delight which facilitates the spiritual struggle for emancipation from existence.

The human level of existence and the six heavenly planes above it are called the *kāma dhātus*, the "worlds of desire." Here the denizens (including, of course, ourselves) are subject to various passions and attachments which, at the lower levels, bring a mixture of pleasure and pain but at the higher bring only sensuous delight. Even where pain is not part of the program, however, these realms are not really satisfactory because one's sojourn there is temporary and pleasure comes to an end.

Above the seven planes of the *kāma dhātus* we find the regions called the *rūpa dhātus*, or "realms of form." It is to these regions that those beings will be reborn who have attained mastery of appropriate trance stages on earth and have consequently purged themselves of the grosser sorts of desire. These are regions the inhabitants of which still possess form or shape and are still subject to certain kinds of relatively refined desire, but their materiality is highly attenuated and physical need is largely absent. In most versions of the system there are sixteen such levels, often referred to as Brahma heavens, although as many as eighteen are sometimes indicated.

Finally, above the *rūpa dhātus* we find the *arūpa dhātus*

—the "formless worlds" or "regions." Here life remains, but form and matter have vanished. There are four of these levels, and at the highest of them a state is enjoyed which is beyond mere consciousness: it is neither consciousness nor unconsciousness but beyond any categories we may use. This level is attained when one has mastered the "four formless meditations" and grasped with mystical clarity the infinity of space, the infinity of consciousness, nothingness, and the state of neither perception nor nonperception.

It may be worth noting that in addition to these realms Mahāyāna Buddhism discusses an infinite number of Buddha *ksetras* (*khettas*), or "Buddha-fields," which are regions of special enlightenment to which the appropriate kind of faith or accomplishment enables a Buddhist to be born. In these regions one's attainment of enlightenment is assured.

We have, then, a multilevel cosmos in which our world and its entourage of heavens and hells is repeated infinitely.

A universe passes through certain stages and is finite in duration. After it arises there is a period of relative stability, then one of deterioration into chaos, then one of renovation. During the descent into chaos there is great destruction, but what is destroyed is not the *dharma* process or the natural elements but only the formations that result from the interaction of these. The *Dīgha Nikāya* contains an interesting picture of the decay of a world:

> Here there is not a total destruction of the earth consequent upon its corruption, but only deterioration to an unbelievably low point before the ensuing improvement sets in. At this lowest point human life is only ten years long and a woman is married at five years. Food is coarse and

scarce. The good old customs are neglected. Sexual prom-
iscuity abounds, including the sexual use of animals. But
seeing the evil of their ways, human beings repent and
amend their conduct. As they begin to practice the virtues
again, life, health, and wealth increase. The life span
doubles to twenty years, twenty years to forty, until at
the apex.[8]

Nirvāna

At the end of this discussion of the Theravādin analysis
of reality we must turn to a subject in which less precision
is possible than anywhere else: *Nirvāna.*

Nirvāna[9] is the name given to the goal of all Buddhist
striving. It serves the emotional function of heaven or
paradise in some other religions, but, like the Christian
heaven, it is a complex idea not to be thought of naïvely as
a place. A Buddhist wants to attain *Nirvāna,* and if he is
a simpleminded person, he will have a correspondingly
simple idea of what it is he seeks, but we are concerned
with philosophy. For the Buddhist philosopher what is
this ultimate attainment?

Nirvāna is unconditioned. In this it is distinguished from
all that can be said merely to "exist." It is therefore as far
beyond existence as it is beyond non-existence, and since
our language and our logic are themselves based upon our
experience of existence, *Nirvāna* is beyond thought or expression. Nevertheless something can be said, even if in-
adequately and only as a sort of circumnavigation of the
subject.

In Buddhist thought to be unconditioned means to be
free from three marks or limitations which haunt everything we know. It means to be free from impermanence,
disturbance (or suffering), and dependence upon or dan-

ger from any source within or outside oneself. It follows
that the man who has attained *Nirvāna*, liberated as he is
from these marks, cannot be said to exist (since our use
of this word is tied to the marks of conditioned existence)
and cannot be said not to exist. The very category "existence" is no longer relevant to describe his state.

As *Nirvāna* is not a place, neither is it a mere state of
mind, for it is an ultimate liberation that transcends the
very notion of "mind." It is the condition in which passion
and ignorance are extingushed, but in their place there is
no mere vacuum. *Nirvāna* is not an annihilation but an
overcoming of all that conditions and limits; it could not
be described adequately by any metaphor, but the Buddhists were fond of likening it to fire. For this comparison
to illumine us, however, we must remember that those who
used it in India believed that fire was one of the basic
elements and utterly indestructible. When fire "went out,"
it did not go in any direction or to any place in the world,
and it did not cease to be: it simply returned to its
mysterious and unperceivable source. So the enlightened
man who died was extinguished; thus he attained *Nirvāna*.
He was not annihilated, but he no longer existed—he was
like fire, indestructible but no longer manifest in the
phenomenal world and in no condition or state that our
minds could imagine. The *dharmas* would no longer come
together to construct for him a body, since *Nirvāna* is
deliverance from that necessity, but nothing has perished
except the illusion of his individual, concrete, and endur-
ingly self-sustained selfhood. As the scripture has it:
"There is no measure to him who has gone to rest; he
keeps nothing that could be named. When all *dharmas*
are abolished, all paths of speech are also abolished." [10]

In the concept of *Nirvāna*, then, we have not only the

goal of the Buddhist life but the attempt to name that which is *true*, that which *is*. To attain *Nirvāna* is not simply to know the Truth but to be the Truth. In this way it begins to loom increasingly in Theravāda writings in the shape of an absolute, yet the Theravādins in general have always preferred not to press the subject. Their *abhidharma* analysis concentrates on conditioned existence almost exclusively, and this appears as a realistic pluralism. Since *Nirvāna* is inexpressible, it is not really developed as a philosophical idea. Yet there are some suggestive passages of scripture, and one in particular which seems to promise so much that one wonders at its neglect:

> There is, O disciples, an unborn, not become, not compounded, not constructed. If there were not this unborn, not become, not compounded, not constructed, no escape could be seen from here from that which is born, become, compounded, constructed.[11]

Similarly, the twenty-sixth *sutta* of the *Majjhima Nikāya* describes the object of Buddhist striving as that which is unborn, unaging, undecaying, undying, unsorrowing, and unstained. This is *Nirvāna*, but such a way of describing it raises questions for which Theravādins have not usually been concerned to provide answers. If an escape is possible from what is born, what is it that escapes? Obviously not an imperishable self, for that has been consistently denied. In what way is the universe of conditioned *dharmas* related to this unborn reality? Is *Nirvāna* wholly other than our world? Mahāyāna critics have frequently accused their Theravādin cousins of such a dualism, but then what is the ground of conditioned existence and how could escape be possible in it? Are *Nirvāna* and the world really identical? That, surely, is hard to reconcile with the radical

difference between the conditioned world as Theravāda
describes it and the unconditioned *Nirvāna.* There are
nagging questions here, but the Theravādin may remember that the Buddha himself declined to answer some
questions on the ground that the answer would not be
understood until the questioner had enjoyed full enlightenment and the question itself had therefore become irrelevant. In the meantime, to pursue the question that cannot
be answered in terms of our experience is to waste our time
and energy, both of which should be devoted to eagerly
pursuing the explicit disciplines of Buddhism.[12]

But some questions still nag, and as the Mahāyānists
long ago broke out of the abhidharmic confinement to deal
with them, so today some Theravādins are speaking in
tones not quite like those of their predecessors. Some, for
instance, seem to be turning toward a sort of idealism—
or at least mentalism—which prejudices the apparently
realistic concept of *dharmas* in orthodox writing.[13] But the
most energetic attempts to grapple with the kind of problem we have raised have so far been within the Mahāyāna
schools of Buddhism, and these we must next consult.
Meanwhile, let us note that *Nirvāna* has emerged as the
single ground of enduring value: but it is a value which
disvalues all that does not serve it.

MAHĀYĀNA

Mahāyāna may be said to begin its own metaphysics
with a rejection of the very foundation of Theravāda's:
the "own-being" or self-existence and substantiality of the
dharmas. The notion of these real but fleeting point-instants was useful enough as a way of picturesquely describing the transience of all existent things, but if taken

too seriously, it seemed to impute a kind of solidity or autonomy to the world that Mahāyānists believed was inappropriate. Why, they asked, should one stop one's analysis of the insubstantiality of things so arbitrarily at the *dharmas?* Why not recognize that this is no logical terminus for the critical acids of a truly Buddhist investigation? Thus a school of Buddhist philosophy arose that applied its analytical formula to every proposition, Buddhist or other, about existence, and reached, at last, the rejection of all phenomenal substantiality, as well as the rejection of any nihilistic view of existence. Our examination of the Mahāyāna metaphysics must begin with a glance at the logical procedures of this school—the Mādhyamika. We shall see that although Mahāyāna Buddhism has, in its long history, contained many sects or schools, two of these have been most formatively significant for its philosophy: the Mādhyamika and the Yogācāra. The latter we shall consider shortly.

Mādhyamika

The early Mādhyamikans were dialecticians who operated with a form of logical analysis which can, for our purposes, be conveniently simplified. There are, they said, four alternative possibilities facing every proposition, and these are:

1. Being, or Affirmation
2. Non-being, or Negation
3. Both Being and Non-being (affirmation and negation)
4. Neither Being nor Non-being (affirmation nor negation)

Normally one may expect to adopt one of these as the status of a proposition in logic or of an entity in existence. As an illustration of the use of this formula let us consider the ancient problem of the relation of cause and effect. The Sāmkhya philosophers were adherents of what, in our formula, may be called Position No. 1: they argued that effect and cause are identical and things are therefore self-becoming or self-caused. The Theravādins are advocates of Position No. 2, since they argue that effect is different from cause. The Jains held Position No. 3 and said that cause and effect are both different and identical, since there is both a continuous and an emergent aspect in the arising of an effect. Finally, there are the skeptics who say that the relation of cause and effect is neither identity nor difference, properly speaking, since in fact there is no causal relation at all, no cause or effect to discuss, and things simply "occur" by chance. Theirs is Position No. 4. We may summarize these positions thus:

Sāmkhya	a is b
Theravāda	a is not b
Jain	a is and is not b
Skeptic	a neither is nor is not b

Having thus stipulated all the apparent available possibilities in a discussion of cause and effect, the Mādhyami-kans then proceeded to examine each of the alternatives and to discover why it was rejected by the advocates of the others. The Sāmkhya view is vulnerable because it cannot even be discussed without cause and effect being verbally separated, thus implying their difference even as their identity is being affirmed. The Theravāda view also fails because if the effect is different from the cause, it is hard to see on what grounds it arises at all—that is, an effect which is not identical with its cause in some sense cannot really be an effect of that cause at all. Out of complete otherness and discontinuity no fruit can come (for although familiarity may breed contempt, it takes a certain amount of familiarity to breed anything!). But even the Jains have not solved the problem, according to Mādhyamikans, because they argue that a cause has two different aspects (identity with its effect and non-identity) and it is an ancient principle of Buddhist logic that anything divided among conflicting characteristics cannot be regarded as one. Thus the aspect of the cause that is identical to the effect becomes one thing, and the aspect that is different becomes another, and the entire proposition has broken down as we no longer have one cause, or the one cause has been destroyed by division. Finally, if the skeptic advances a reason for his position, he thereby denies it, since reason and conclusion are merely other forms of cause and effect. If he does not advance a reason, he has, in effect, withdrawn from contention.

The result of this analysis is the inevitable conclusion that *no* proposition really discloses the relation of cause and effect, but not (let it be noted) that there is no such relation. Every position, including that of the skeptic, has been shown (at least to Mādhyamikan satisfaction) to be inadequate and the only possible conclusion is that Truth must be inexpressible and beyond all logical categories.

Now let us apply this sort of analysis to the *dharmas*. If these are really point-instants, each passing away utterly as it is replaced by a new one, so that no continuity, no enduring essence, passes from one to another, we have genuine otherness between all *dharmas*. They are isolated instants. But, as we have seen, such a radical separation means that there can be no explicable world process because there can be no cause-effect relation. Even if the Theravādins try to be faithful to Gautama by ingeniously or ingenuously tying their *dharma* theory to his theory of dependent co-production (which is a strong causal system), the result must be unconvincing. The *dharmas* simply cannot provide the ground for an understanding of the world as an eternal becoming. One may say, in fact, that the Mādhyamikans placed two opposed theories in dialectical tension in their discussion of the Real:

| Monist Traditions (e.g., Vedānta) | *versus* | Pluralist Traditions (e.g., Theravāda) |

Whereas in Hegelian dialectic this antithesis would be expected to produce a synthesis, for the Mādhyamikans the result was the rejection of both alternatives, and of any synthesis which might develop. Theravāda pluralism cannot account for the world, for instance, because of the separation of the basic elements (*dharmas*) and the consequent failure of any productive relationship to develop. But monism also fails because if the Real is genuinely and simply One, there can be no production of an Other. Yet we perceive a world of otherness. If one said that the world was mere illusion, he would still have to answer the question: Is this illusion real? If it is real, then one no longer has monism, for the One has Another (the illusion) beside it; but if the illusion is not real, it must be . . . an illusion! And from the idea of an illusion of an illusion one falls into a hopelessly infinite regress. The truth about Reality, then, must be not One, not Many—in fact, it must be inexpressible.

Lesser men might well have succumbed to a *de facto* nihilism after living with Mādhyamikan analysis, but two things prevented this from happening to the Buddhists.

One was the simple fact that nihilism had been shown as inadequate as any other position they examined; the other was their religious experience in the context of Buddhist meditational disciplines. They had known the moment of awakening to Something that transcended the world: their logic had taught them that this Something was, in fact, *no thing*, since it could not be categorized or expressed, but that it was not *nothing*, since nihilism was not a tenable position. There was, then, a Real and it was not simply the world *as one usually understood it;* it could be known only when one had abandoned all the logical presuppositions with which one became burdened from infancy. It could be known through religious discipline, but Mādhyamikan logic could also help by chopping down, one by one, all the false conceptions with which one customarily interpreted the data of experience, leaving one mentally naked and defenseless so that Truth might make its surprising appearance. For our problem is not so much that we have to learn the Truth as that we have to unlearn error. The Truth simply is, and when ignorance and error are gone, the Truth alone remains.

But the repetition of Mādhyamikan logic and the use of meditational techniques did not alone satisfy those Buddhists who, in increasing numbers, found themselves alienated from the Theravādins and other so-called Hīnayāna schools. If Truth is inexpressible, nevertheless there may be words that can awaken us to it. Of course one must never take the words too seriously, but perhaps something can be said about Truth which will at least turn a mind in the correct direction to find it. It is with the attempt to use such words, despite their limitations, that we shall now concern ourselves, for this is the essential function, in Mahāyāna, of philosophy.

Śūnyatā

In the important little *Heart Sūtra* it is said: "Avalokita, the Holy Lord and *Bodhisattva,* was moving in the deep course of the Wisdom which has gone beyond. He looked down from on high, he beheld but five heaps, and he saw that in their own-being they were empty." [14] There is so much implied in this short verse that a book might well be written to expound it. Avalokita is one of the great legendary semi-divine figures in Mahāyāna, and we are told here that in the state of transcendental wisdom he looked at the five *skandhas* of which all life is composed and detected that in their essence they were "empty." The word "empty" (*śūnya*) has two major significations in this text, the first being virtually a denial of Theravāda *dharma* theory, and the second being the affirmation of a theme that was to become central to Mahāyāna. In the first place it means that the *skandhas* are without substance and are not self-arising (that is, they lack aseity). They do not come into existence because of anything inherent in their particularity. Thus they cannot serve as the end point of the erosive analysis to which Buddhism submits existent reality.

Secondly, our sentence means that in their essence the *skandhas* are the *Empty*—the Void (*Śūnyatā*). That is to say, they are that which is empty of all that can be discriminated and categorized and reduced to descriptive propositions. They are, in their true center, beyond all dualities. In a word, in essence they are that mysterious and indefinable Reality to which Mādhyamikan logic had pointed but which it could not name. The multiplicity of *skandhas* and *dharmas* is thus denied substance and self-sustained existence *as a multiplicity,* for the unique and indivisible Reality of them all is not *many* (although it encompasses the many) but the Absolute, which is beyond definition or description. This is, no doubt, a rather difficult idea, but we must remember that Mādhyamikan logic had forewarned us by showing that there is a Truth of reality which eludes all possible propositions and which must, therefore, be hacked at by verbal strokes that are always doomed to miss clarity or their target—Reality—or both.

Since ultimate Reality is devoid of anything that could give us a proper conceptual handle (it does not conform to any of our categories including existence and non-existence, universality or particularity) it will be convenient, as the Mahāyānists found, to refer to it as *Śūnyatā,* the Void. *Behind the* dharmas, *which are now seen as no more final than the* skandhas *that they compose, lies* Śūnyatā, *not as a reality separate from them, not as divided among them, but as the essentially undivided Reality that appears to our senses as divided particularity.*

That we call the mysterious essence of all things a "Void" should not be held to imply that it is literally vacant; it means simply that what is finally real is without (void of) limitations such as form, dimension, number, color, and so on. We are not talking here about a gigantic lump of substance out of which everything is made, for *Śūnyatā* is infinite and, as we have said, indivisible, which means that there is nothing outside it, and it is not partly present in one thing and partly in another. However much this discomforts logic, we must say that it is the reality of whatever is yet in being; thus it is never divided. The Mahāyānists felt that their logic might drive one to such a perception, but never that it could express it or actually create the vision of Truth.

So many and desperate were the attempts to give at least approximate expression to what was held here to be the Truth that a great number of synonyms for *Śūnyatā* came to be used, each providing its own gleam of light, but none finally more adequate than "Void." It may be useful and suggestive simply to list a few of the more important of these without much attempt at present to explore the range of their significance.

> *Satyatā:* The True
> *Bhūtatā:* The Real
> *Dharmadhātu:* The Realm of Truth
> *Dharmakāya:* The Body of Truth
> *Svabhāvakāya:* The "Own-Nature" Body (implying aseity)
> *Tathatā:* Thusness or Suchness (the inner reality of things)
> *Samatā:* Sameness (in which there are really no discriminable distinctions)
> *Anutpāda:* The Unborn (as distinct from that which comes into and eventually leaves existence)

The list could be extended to many times its length, but these examples will serve to show the kind of thought that is struggling for words. For convenience we will usually refer to the Mahāyāna ultimate as *Śūnyatā*.

One thing is clear: from the realistic pluralism of Theravāda we have now moved to an absolutism of a very radical sort. *Śūnyatā* is in no sense an entity beside others; it is not like God, with whom one may seek to be united or in whom we seek to lose ourselves, for *Śūnyatā* means precisely that there is no duality to overcome, no real division of self and other. As we shall see, there will be constant pressure to transform this absolutism into an idealism.

Our discussion of *Śūnyatā* will have something of the character of a whirlpool as we keep circling the inexpressible center. We may begin by describing it negatively in terms made famous by Nāgārjuna, who said that there is in it "neither production nor destruction nor annihilation nor persistence nor unity nor plurality nor coming in nor going out." [15] Like negative theology in the Christian tradition, this is doubtless the most satisfactory way of speaking, since speak we must, of the Ultimate, but it can hardly be said to satisfy most men's longing for understanding.

We may then resort to Nāgārjuna again, this time speaking in a different mood, and say that in its own true realm —in the noumenal sphere as we might say—the Void is an absolute unrestrictedness, beyond comprehension, and that in the phenomenal sphere there is, consequently, nothing finally "real" about particularity and difference. Indeed, he says, "If thou thinkest that things exist on account of their self-essence [*svabhāva*, i.e., they are self-caused, self-sustaining, self-sufficient], then thou seest that they come out of causelessness." [16] What Nāgārjuna is saying here is that if anything is self-derived, it is without a cause beyond itself, and we see, in fact, nothing that cannot be shown to have an external cause; thus nothing in the phenomenal world conforms to this image of self-causation. Even a cursory glance at things reveals that they do not arise by means of their own power since a cause beyond them can always be discovered, and this certainly suggests that the entire world of separate entities is a world of contingency. If so, where shall we find that which is non-contingent and which is therefore capable of giving rise to and sustaining the world? Nāgārjuna's thought, at times, seems strikingly similar to Thomas Aquinas' argu-

ment that God must exist because a wholly contingent
world is not self-explanatory.

The Void, then, is the ground of all existential becoming,
yet in itself it is beyond all coming and going. It is
dynamic, yet there is neither production nor destruction
within its own essence. It *is* the many items of our experience, and it is perfect and undivided unity in its essence—and because it is both multiplicity and unity it is
"really" neither, but eludes both categories. Above all, it
is not, as we have said, some store of immutable substance.
One may even grasp part of the meaning of *Śūnyatā* by
saying that the universe is a network of dependently co-
arising phenomena, and *Śūnyatā* is precisely that network
of relationship.

At this point we had better bring our train of thought
out of the tunnel for a moment and into a patch of sunlight. There is an ancient legend that is used sometimes to
try to picture the Void and if we do not take it too seriously, it may help to illuminate a little what we have been
saying. The great god Indra is supposed to have had a
marvelous net, fashioned from precious stones. Such was
the character of these highly reflective gems and of the
net they composed, that if a man looked into one stone, he
saw mirrored there every other. Each stone seemed to be
at once uniquely itself and the entire net. In a similar way
we may say that the particular mundane entity exists; it
is no mere illusion, but to see it as it really is in its "suchness" is to see it as *Śūnyatā*, the reality of all things. Not,
we must emphasize endlessly, a piece of *Śūnyatā*, for that
would be an absurd idea (the dividing of the indivisible),
but *Śūnyatā* itself. Each entity, every relationship, all are
present in every item of existence, yet the world is not
therefore unreal. Where some Indian thought tends to melt

the many into the One, Mahāyāna's aim is to show the One flowing into the many without thereby being divided.

Another change of metaphor may help—within limits. Devotees of the *Avatamsaka Sūtra* are fond of describing the relationship between the Absolute and our world of particular entities as similar to that between the waves and the ocean. Each wave appears as a separate being, yet the reality of each is the same ocean. The problem with this image is, of course, that a wave consists of a mere part of the ocean at any given moment and we should not infer that the Absolute is similarly divided among existents.

The truth of the universe—the Truth that is *Śūnyatā*—is, then, one that somehow embraces both sameness and difference without diminishing either. This is sometimes discussed in terms of what are called the "six-fold characteristics of Being," in which it is affirmed that existence reveals the following features:

1. Unity (the many are One)
2. Diversity (each entity is itself alone)
3. Harmony (the various entities combine to form the whole as the walls, floor, ceiling, roof, etc., of a building constitute the entire house)
4. Difference (each entity has its own function)
5. Formative characteristic (that is, there is a power in Being to bring about formation much as a house is formed by the joining of its parts)
6. Self-preservation (nothing loses its identity or performs the function of something else)[17]

Up to this point, it should be clear, we have been busily engaged in putting together a collection of ideas that tend to find each other uncongenial company: unity and diversity, harmony and difference, production and non-production, universality and particularity, to name but a few. If we were trying to build a coherent concept, we should certainly have failed, but we knew from the outset that Mahāyāna, insofar as it is faithful to the Mādhyamika side of its heritage, recognizes that the Absolute defies all coherent statements. The function of our discordant ideas, then, is not to build upon each other, but by denying each other to establish a propositional structure that leads our thought without ever allowing us to suppose that a clear proposition is the Truth. This is a mode of philosophical statement which is self-negating and is designed to serve the purpose of goading thought on to a point at which it realizes its own insufficiency, but realizes it (and thereupon resorts to other Buddhist disciplines) with no mere vacuum but with some substratum of conviction remaining. But perhaps this purpose has not been sufficiently served yet in our exposition, so we shall make another swing around our whirlpool.

We have seen that Gautama taught a doctrine of *anātman* (*anattā*)—he denied the presence in us of an eternal and immutable self. In Theravāda this was generally taken to mean that apart from the *skandhas* there is no enduring ego, but with the advent of Mahāyāna absolutism the discussion took a slight turn. The permanent individual ego was still denied, but now it is clear that something expressing itself in me does indeed endure and is immortal—the Void. Soon the Absolute Reality began to be spoken of as if it were a cosmic Self, rather like the Vedāntic *Ātman* in at least some important respects. It was argued that Gautama had meant by *anātman* that no particular entity, such as a man, has an ego or a soul of its own, but there is indeed one—and only one—authentic Self, namely, *Śūnyatā*, the *Dharmakāya*. A modern Mahāyāna philosopher will sometimes explain that Gautama was not really interested in metaphysics and tried merely to teach the way of deliverance from suffering. What he said, therefore, should be understood not ontologically but merely as an imperative. When he says that there is no self, he means "do not trust in a separate, self-sufficient, immortal soul of your own." There is no profit in hoping that you possess an inherently immortal self which shall rise out of the body at death. What he did *not* necessarily mean is that there is *no* immortality concealed within existence.

Yamakami Sōgen argues that the Buddha attacked the *Ātman* idea in order to disabuse the eternalists of their false hope of personal immortality; but he spoke repeatedly *as if* men had an ego to those who, he felt, were in danger of slipping into nihilism. The truth is not literally and exactly either of these disavowed positions, or the simple denial of them. What Gautama is very concerned to renounce is the idea of the *hinātman*, the individual soul as an independent entity with "the power of existing apart from the body and of directing all its activities." [18] But when this error has been safely disposed of, another concept of Selfhood emerges: "While condemning, as rank heresy, the theories of a Universal Creator and of an individual soul, Buddhism not only acknowledges the permanence of the noumenal *ego*, but actually enjoins its adherents to train themselves in such a manner as to be able to attain union with the Great Soul of the Universe, the technical term for which is *mahātman*." [19]

Now, the *mahātman* of which Yamakami Sōgen speaks is none other than *Śūnyatā*, and he renders us the valuable service of making clear yet another area in which the ubiquity of this Absolute is manifest. Yet his manner of expression is dangerously misleading in one respect. To speak of attaining union with something surely implies an original separation, an authentic otherness which must be overcome. What, in fact, the enlightened man comes to know is that he has never really been other than the Truth. *Śūnyatā* is what is, and this is one reason for the continuing Mahāyāna belief that their Absolute is not really the Vedāntic *Ātman* in disguise. The Vedāntist, it is argued, longs for and is deeply attached to the infinite Cosmic Self which is alternatively known as Brahman or *Ātman*, but the Mahāyānist knows that such attachment is error. He *is* the Absolute: to what, then, could he be attached? It is the dispelling of illusion about himself (about his Self), not the attainment of a union or a status he lacks that the Mahāyānist endorses. Whether this is a fair assault on Vedānta or not is at present irrelevant; it helps us to see how the Buddhist views his own position.

Śūnyatā, then, is the Real, manifest in every particular entity without being divided. This idea appears illogical—and, indeed, it is. But the Christian idea of a God who is emphatically *one* and utterly indivisible yet who is known as a trinity of *personae* (Father, Son, and Holy Spirit) is no less illogical. The problem we encounter in understanding either of these complex ideas arises from the fact that our language is based on experience of finite entities which cannot ever be found occupying more than a limited and measurable single space in any given moment of time. But *Śūnyatā* and God are unique in their infinitude and we have no logic of infinity. Finite objects cannot be in two places at one time without division, but the infinite is not bound by space or time, and actually transcends the distinction between places and times. Consequently it can be you and I; it can be Tom Jones yesterday and Tom Jones tomorrow—and all without change in its essence.

The Mahāyāna Absolute, then, is the Real, and the speculation about *dharmas* as separate point-instants becomes virtually irrelevant. Each *dharma* would be no other than *Śūnyatā;* each *skandha* is the same. Each person is the Absolute. So instead of an elaborate *dharma* analysis we have the affirmation of a *Dharmakāya*—a *Dharma* body —the Void, the Suchness of all real things: in short, we have one comprehensive *Dharma* thoroughly deserving of a capital *D*.

Similarly, the separate moments of time now become each the Absolute expressed temporally. A second is eternity without ceasing also to be that particular second. Thus the entire history of the universe is fully present in an unending Now, yet it is also true that this moment is unique and arises in dependence on all other moments that have preceded it.

Again, there can be no real separation of the wisdom (*prajñā*) that intuits the Real and the latter itself. "Knowledge [reason] and its object [the Real] coincide; there is non-duality. . . . This too is *Śūnyatā*." [20] That is to say, when we reach awareness of ultimate Truth, knowing and being are one. This means that the awakening of the Buddha is the Absolute (*Dharma*) awakening to itself— and that the Awakening itself is also the Absolute!

Mādhyamikan logic and Buddhist religious experience have, then, led us to an Absolute which, in many respects, is justly described as monistic. But the Buddhist does not like the epithet "monist" because he associates this with Indian Vedānta philosophy and feels that he is offering a point of view with some important differences. In Vedānta,

for instance, when the ultimate Truth (Brahman) is realized the world of particularity is seen as essentially *maya*
—"illusion." For the Mahāyānist there is also illusion, but
this consists (at least for the Mādhyamikan tradition) of
a deluded manner of seeing and valuing the world; the
world itself is not simply illusory but is actually the expression of the Real, and as such is also real even though
not self-originated or self-sustaining in its particularities.
Logic breaks down when it attempts to deal with the
status of the individual entities of the world in relation to
the Absolute. You are *Śūnyatā* and so am I, yet *Śūnyatā*
is not divided any more than you are me or I am you. Our
relationship, if we should influence each other, is an "in-
terpenetration of Absolutes" yet there is but one Absolute.
Mādhyamika philosophy would prefer to live with these
irreducible inconsistencies of expression than impute mere
fantasy value to the world.

Further, monism suggests to the Buddhist a very static
view of the Real. Brahman, he contends, has always really
appeared in Indian thought (other than Buddhist) as essentially unmoved and unmoving, so that events *must* be
regarded as illusion; *Śūnyatā*, on the other hand, although
unchanging in essence is constantly expressing itself in the
events and entities of the world. Another illogicality cheer-
fully borne.

To have such difficulties with logic, however, even when
they are sustained by a Mādhyamikan demonstration of the
inability of any logical form to comprehend Reality, is
tantalizing to many philosophers and it is not surprising
that a rival school of thought arose which accepted the
Śūnyatā idea but attempted to give it a rather more com-
prehensible and reasonable form. This school is known
historically as the Yogācāra, or the Vijñānavāda school,

and its modification of *Śūnyatā* in the direction of idealism must be described briefly.

Yogācāra

A Mādhyamika philosopher is rather like a tightrope walker. He moves precariously between the chasms of nihilism and naïve realism, a false step easily involving him in denying any authenticity to the world or, on the other side, in affirming the world as existing by its own right. Perhaps the delicacy of this position led some to seek a broader path which would still preserve what they regarded as essential. In addition, there was certainly the persistent siren serenade of Indian idealism constantly luring the Buddhists back toward the familiar currents of Vedāntic[21] speculation. And there was the irritating persistence of illogicalities that Mādhyamika found inevitable but which some men found intolerable.

Again, Mādhyamikans had contended that the basic human problem was false discrimination. We habitually impute substantiality to existents when, in fact, they have no self-sustaining authenticity of their own. But how, then, does illusion arise? The illusion, like the Truth, must in some mysterious way be *Śūnyatā*, yet it is a kind of *un*-truth. How can there be error? Mādhyamikans did not pursue this question with much diligence, and here was another cause for dissatisfaction with that school.

In time, then, a new sect arose, which came to be called the Yogācāra, eagerly attacking the questions left alone by Mādhyamika and building on the basis of the *Śūnyatā* concept a structure that they hoped would be more coherent and complete. Perhaps we can most conveniently begin our discussion of them by setting out the shape of

Yogācāra psychology; we shall then be able to see easily how, according to this school, error comes to rule our thought. Let us first outline diagrammatically the elements of this psychology and then offer an explanation.

We are already familiar with the functions of the six sense *vijñānas* from the Theravāda psychology. They are consciousness arising from sense experience, or from the

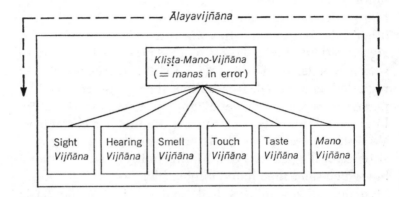

activity of mentation which is also regarded as a sensory phenomenon. In Yogācāra theory this sensory experience occurs as an activity within *Śūnyatā* which, however, is now called the *Ālayavijñāna*—"store consciousness." Here is a new interpretation of the Absolute which deserves close attention.

An earlier school, the Sautrantikas, in discussing the law of action and effect (*karma*) had reasoned that the effects of deeds are like seeds which are carried in the stream of experience until they ripen as the fruit of the original act. Similarly, the Yogācāra philosophers said that all deeds and ideas are like seeds stored and waiting to be brought forth and they named this vast collection the *Ālayavijñāna*. Now, *vijñāna* means "consciousness" and the implication was very clear that events and things in the empirical world are therefore the fruit of a consciousness, that is, they are really the ideas or imaginings of a kind of cosmic awareness. *Ālayavijñāna,* consequently, sometimes is translated "creative imagination." The point is that the Absolute is no longer entirely "void" but has a quite nameable character: it is a store of ideas, and by the time the *Lankāvatāra Sūtra* and *Avatamsaka Sūtra* came to be written, it was also thought of as Mind.

The Yogācāra school found itself now in some measure of opposition to both Hīnayānists (Theravādin and other) and Mādhyamikans, for they argued that the *Ālayavijñāna* is *real* with no equivocation. It does not linger in an elusive realm beyond existence and non-existence. On the other hand, the *Ālayavijñāna alone* is real and all else, including *dharmas,* must be its ideas.

In the earliest form of Yogācāra psychology, before the *Ālayavijñāna* came to be called Mind, it was thought of as a series of seeds waiting for fruition, all of them pure and undefiled. With its hardening into the concept of a cosmic Mind the additional idea developed that it contained not only the pure but also the impure seeds which were the result of karmically bad action.

Between the *Ālayavijñāna* and the sense *vijñānas* there stood the *Klista-Mano-Vijñāna,* or "soiled-mind consciousness," which is, in effect, a false self-consciousness resulting from a loss of sight of the *Ālaya* and the assumption that the *manas,* or function of mentation in its individual form, is a real, permanent ego. *Manas,* receiving the impressions from the sensory *vijñānas* and building concepts from them, finally conceptualizes the individual self and erects this in place of the *Ālayavijñāna,* or true cosmic Self. Here is the manner in which illusion arises and our task is there-

fore to discourage the impure ideas planted by mistaken
manas and to cultivate with discipline the pure ideas that
exist as seeds within the *Ālaya*. This means, in practice, to
abandon false ego satisfactions and desires and allow the
Truth, which is the *Ālayavijñāna*, to dominate our subjectivity as it should.

There seems, for a time, to have been a controversy
within Yogācāra ranks as to whether the *Ālayavijñāna*
should be thought of individualistically or cosmically, but
it is the latter version that survived in strength, and this is
therefore the only form of the theory which we need consider now.

In Yogācāra we find a clear idealism (whether it considered the Real to be "Mind Only" or "Ideas Only") and
no longer much ground for confusion about whether the
world of particular entities was real or not: it was real as
the projection of the *Ālayavijñāna*, just as thoughts are real
as the projections of mentation, but it had no reality within
itself whatever. Although it may not be a pure Yogācāra
work, the *Lankāvatāra Sūtra* is so heavily influenced by
this school, and so readily available to us in a good English
translation by the late D. T. Suzuki, that it may serve
as an introduction of unusual excellence. A few sample
quotations from it will emphasize the idealistic quality of
its, and Yogācāra's, thought:

Again, Mahamati, by the wise the five *skandhas* are regarded as thought-constructions. . . . They are like varieties of forms and objects in a vision, like images and persons in a dream.[22]

Again, Mahamati, my teaching consists in the cessation of
sufferings arising from the discrimination of the triple
world; in the cessation of ignorance, desire, greed, and

causality; and in the recognition that an objective world, like a vision, is the manifestation of Mind itself.[23]

But perhaps the most famous and extraordinary statement of this entire *sūtra*, and the most perfect expression of the logical terminus of Yogācāra impulses, is this:

There is neither a speaker nor speaking nor emptiness since the Mind is seen:

There is no rising of the causal [chain], nor are there any sense-organs; no *dhātus*, no *skandhas*, no greed, no sanskrita.

There is no primarily working fire, no working done, no effects produced, no final limit, no power, no deliverance, no bondage.

There is no state of being to be called neutral; there is no duality of *dharma* and *adharma;* there is no time, no Nirvana, no *dharma*-essence.

And there are no Buddhas, no truths, no fruition, no causal agents, no perversion . . . no passing away, no birth. . . .

I declare [there is] Mind-only.[24]

It did not take Mādhyamikans long to respond to the reasoning we have just examined. Among their criticisms they said that the Vijñānavādins had distorted the scriptures because the texts which seemed to speak of the reality of Mind were offered by the Buddha only as a sop to those people yet unable to grasp the naked Truth. They were a means to bring people to the pure *Śūnyatā* doctrine, and no more. Further, the Yogācāra adept had really abandoned the Middle Way of the Buddha in the acceptance of the real existence of *vijñāna* and the denial of reality (except as idea) to objects; the truth about Reality transcends both "is" and "is not," both existence and non-existence.

More seriously, they argued, if the Absolute is thought
of as Mind, we have a new logical dilemma, and this time
one that is not necessitated by the Truth. Since enlightenment is the Absolute's self-awakening, it becomes difficult
to speak of it if we must do so in terms of a Mind cognizing
itself, for minds may be conscious of objects but never of
themselves.

Indeed, the dependence of a mind upon the objects it
cognizes is obvious. If objects have no reality apart from
Mind, if there is nothing that can meet and provoke Mind
to action, how does the Mind know anything at all? Surely
"Mind" is an inappropriate metaphor at best for discussing
that absolutely real and ubiquitous Void.[25]

One may summarize many of the Mādhyamikan objections by saying that in virtually reducing ontology to
epistemology the Yogācārins had only become imprecise
and had substituted a way of speaking of Absolute Reality
which was more vulnerable to misunderstanding and over-
simplification than the Mādhyamikan refusal to postulate
anything definitive about Śūnyatā.

Despite such attacks and counterattacks the two schools
flourished and may be said to have complemented each
other in the development of the broad Mahāyāna stream of
thought. In later schools the options they represent appeared in strangely interwoven ways, sometimes as an emphasis in one school over against another, sometimes as
strands, not always perfectly harmonized, in a single
school. The Tendai sect, for instance, has been predomi-
nantly Mādhyamikan in their insistence that all phenomena have Absolute Reality whereas the Kegon school has
been Yogācārin in its teaching that Mind is universal and
all phenomena are projections of that Mind. Zen has re-
vealed, in its philosophical productions, a fascinating

fluctuation between the two and a pleasant and instructive exercise consists of examining the writings of D. T. Suzuki to try to disentangle the Yogācāra and the Mādhyamika influences upon his elegant thought.

Nirvāna

In concluding this study of Mahāyāna concepts of Reality and Value, let us consider the notion of *Nirvāna* which emerged in the context of Mahāyāna's absolutism.

We saw that, for Theravāda, *Nirvāna* is that goal of peace and fulfillment toward which every Buddhist strives. We noted also that there is some precedent for referring to it as an "unborn" as well as an unperishing Reality. In Mahāyāna, *Nirvāna* retains both these aspects, but it now becomes identical with *Śūnyatā* itself. *Nirvāna* is the suchness of all things. A contemporary Buddhist has expressed this idea in a moving way:

> A blossoming flower in Spring is *Nirvāna* [in absolute affirmation]; a falling leaf in Autumn is *Nirvāna* [in absolute affirmation]; a painter busying himself in painting is *Nirvāna* [in absolute affirmation]; a Zen master who makes a "lion's roar" shouting his absolute affirmation of himself even at the moment of being murdered is *Nirvāna*.[26]

All existent things are the Absolute affirming itself absolutely and all, therefore, are already *Nirvāna*. We "lack" *Nirvāna* only in our ignorance, for in our being we are already *Nirvāna* itself. Consequently it is possible to say that this world of transience and suffering—*samsāra* (*samsāra*)—is not an evil place from which we must fly to an exotic paradise. On the contrary, the transition from evil to good, from suffering to peace, is a journey of our inward spirit—of our self to the Self—and in the truest sense *samsāra* is already *Nirvāna*.

Nirvāna, then, because it is in reality the eternal Void, is for Mahāyāna as much as for Theravāda the ground of value. But now it is seen that it does not disvalue anything that is; on the contrary it envalues all because it is the Truth of all. To understand this is to awaken to the wonder of the simplest things and actions and to understand the meaning of the ecstatic T'ang dynasty verse:

> How miraculous! How wonderful!
> I draw water, I carry wood.[27]

V

MAN AND HIS EXISTENCE

Theravāda's concept of the person should already be clear from the discussion in the last chapter, but a brief reiteration of a few points may be useful. We have seen that Buddhism denies the existence of a permanent, substantial self, or ego. This does not mean that it refuses to acknowledge that there is a sense of cohesion and continuity in each of us, a functional gathering and centering of our consciousness. It means that for Buddhism there is no enduring substratum, no transcendent soul in us apart from the five *skandhas*. The empirical "self," or centered consciousness, is itself only an aspect of our skandhic construction and not something that bears the *skandhas*.

Strictly speaking, there is action but no enduring actor; there is knowledge but no knower. There is something resembling a stream of experience or awareness composed of dependent but unsupported discrete moments—it is rather like a river without a riverbed! One of the more colorful statements of this personal egolessness comes to us from an ancient commentary:

The monk, when he moves forwards or backwards, is not

113

like a blind worldling who in his delusion thinks that it
is a self which moves, or that the movement has been produced by a self, as when one says, "I go forwards," or "the
act of going forwards is produced by me." But, free from
delusion, he thinks: "when there arises in the mind the
idea 'I will move forward,' then there arises also, together
with just that idea, a nervous impulse [lit. a process of
oscillation, *vāyodhātu*], which originates from the mind
and generates bodily expression." It is thus that this heap
of bones, which is politely called a "body," moves forwards,
as a result of the diffusion of a nervous impulse due to the
mind. Who then is there the one who walks? To whom does
this walking belong? In the ultimate sense it is the going
of impersonal physical processes [lit. "elements"].[1]

G. P. Malalasekera, a modern authority, expresses the
same idea:

> In life, there is no I that experiences, no I that thinks,
> speaks, does. I do not have these as my functions, but this
> doing, speaking, thinking, itself I am. . . . A man's per-
> sonality is at any given moment a fact [*sacca*], but it does
> not correspond to any fixed entity in man, something that
> persists while all else changes.[2]

Despite this egolessness, the stream of experience that
is "my" life is haunted by *dukkha*—a sense of unfulfillment,
dissatisfaction, alienation from what is, disappointment
and anxiety. In a world of transience and imperfection I
long to have and to be that which is whole and enduring.
Here, then, is the Buddha's first "Noble" (or Aryan)
Truth: birth, decay, death, sorrow, lamentation, pain,
grief, despair, and the failure to fulfill one's hopes produce
in us an inescapable frustration.

The questions that cry out to be answered are these:
What promotes and sustains this stream of awareness, and

how may the suffering it entails be overcome? If we can understand how my apparent individuality comes into seeming existence, and how the skandhic continuum is sustained, we may see how to defeat the dilemma of despair that sooner or later must make any man its victim.

The first great word in our explanation must be *karma* (*kamma*). This means "act" or "deed" but points to the theory that every event, every action, every volition, must have a consequence, good or ill, so that from the seed of a single moment of will a chain reaction is established which is difficult to terminate. As we shall see, the notion of *karma* expanded itself in Buddha's thought into a fairly elaborate causal system, but first we must clearly understand *karma* itself.

Karma

The role that *karma* plays in the human personality can best be approached by means of metaphor. We are very familiar with the somewhat imprecise idea of "character." It is a common understanding that a person's actions, choices, decisions, longings—in short, his volitions—have a formative effect upon what we are pleased to call his character, so that a man of "good character" is presumed to be one who has staunchly chosen to do and to applaud the morally admirable throughout his life. *Karma*, in one of its aspects, is quite like character. It, too, represents the present status of an individual and is the result of past volitions. It would be as true to say of a man that he had bad *karma* as that he had a bad character, for in saying either we mean that he is morally formed by his own past and his responses through it. A difference is that *karma* is not presumed to have begun to operate merely at the time of a particular birth but stretches over many lifetimes in the same stream of becoming to which the present "individual" belongs. Another difference is that one's *karma* operates not only subjectively but objectively: it shapes not only the person but the external circumstances that impinge upon his existence.

Another metaphor may be found in the idea of force. European philosophy has some familiarity with *élan vital* and similar terms, and has known the image of a life force thrusting itself through the phases of evolution toward some transitory moment of present and relative fulfillment. *Karma*, too, can be thought of as a force of which a particular individual is a momentary and unique embodiment —the present consequence of all that has occurred within its stream of karmic energy. But *karma* is not merely a force, it is a coherent one: each moment in its career is shaped firmly by the last. Yet this idea is no naïve determinism, for the individual who is the momentary expression of *karma* must be held to possess the power to adopt a moral or an immoral response to the circumstances which *karma* presents to him, and that response becomes influential for the next karmic moment. This limited power in us is not quite what is usually meant by "free will," for a really "free" will would be outside the realm of karmic conditioning, a conception that introduces a note of chaos into what is, in fact, a very orderly development. Rather we are speaking here of a capacity to become "mindful" (to use a favorite Buddhist word) or sensitively aware of the motives that arise in us, and to allow those motives to stand before the judgment of Buddhist teaching. The encounter of motive and *dharma*, or Truth, may then produce a reaction in the moral chemistry of our skandhic being which directs the force of *karma* along an altered trajectory. The better our karmic direction becomes, of course, the easier it is for us to attain such mindfulness.

Maha Thera U Thittila, in a fine article, uses another metaphor: he likens *karma* to fire. It is the property of fire, he points out, to burn and to give heat. "If we use it properly it gives us light, cooks our food, burns up things we want to destroy—but if we use it wrongly it burns us and our property. It is the nature of fire to burn and it is our responsibility to use it in the right way. . . . In this respect, *kamma* is like fire." [3] In other words, the universe is governed by the law of cause and effect; every event has its consequence. It is for us to use this fact to produce good effects rather than bad. This image, too, has its usefulness, but I think that it is a little too simple (like the others we have used) and runs the risk of making us believe that we are, after all, real egos who can stand apart from and use *karma* as if this were a tool at our disposal. The truth is much more subtle. We are, in this moment, the personification of our *karma*, yet we may bring what we are to the healing light of Buddhist wisdom and there be turned toward more profitable paths.

The concept of *karma*, then, embraces all volitional actions (for only actions that are consciously performed and intended are karmic in consequence) and their fruits in events, circumstances, and characters. We need not conceal the fact that it may be difficult to reconcile the forceful and formative stream of *karma* with the notion of even a limited capacity for volition, yet it is a Buddhist conviction that without volition there is no *karma* and that we are *responsible* for the direction our karmic process follows. It would be false to say either that we are simply

determined in our behavior by karmic pressures or that
we are perfectly free beings gleefully shaping our selves
without restraint.

As we go farther into Theravāda analysis, we find that
karma is susceptible to a fourfold classification, each
category of which possesses subcategories. There is no
point at present in laboring this, but the most important
ideas should be specified:

1. Karma *Classified According to Period of Fulfillment.*
Some kinds of karmic action produce their consequences
during the same lifetime in which they themselves occurred, whereas others produce results in the next lifetime.
A third type produces consequences in even more remote
life periods. In addition there are karmic acts that fail to
produce any evident result because some necessary auxil-
iary cause fails to appear: this is called "ineffective" *karma.*

2. Karma *Classified According to Function.* There is
karma that shapes the circumstances of a future birth and
that is therefore usually called "reproductive" *karma.*
Other *karma* sustains those karmic effects which are
presently operative. In addition, there is *karma* that modifies any present karmic effects, and *karma* that actually
cancels such effects, replacing them with its own.

3. Karma *Classified According to Priority.* Not all actions produce results as striking or as immediate as those
of other actions. Consequently one may say that some
karma is more "weighty" than other *karma;* for instance
the very bad *karma* in such deeds as murder (especially
of a parent or of an enlightened Buddhist) is very weighty
indeed. One's action in the moment of death constitutes a
special category of *karma* which (at least in the absence
of weighty, unexpended *karma*) largely determines the
circumstances of the succeeding birth. One may also speak

of "habitual" *karma*, meaning the typical, commonly repeated actions of an individual and their unexceptional consequences. Whatever *karma* one has yet to expend is sometimes called "reserved" *karma*. All *karma* has consequences, unless necessary attendant circumstances are not present, but the weightier it is the more influential and immediate its results are likely to be.

4. Karma *Classified According to Its Realm*. A final category concerns itself with the level or realm of existence in which the karmic consequences occur, for instance, the realm of desire, of form, of formlessness, and so on. For some further discussion of this subject one may refer to U Thittila's article "The Fundamental Principles of Theravāda Buddhism."

From what has now been said, it may be seen that *karma* is an enormously significant factor in the life of any person. It is, however, a concept sufficiently unfamiliar to most Westerners that it may be profitable for us to pause at this point to consider a Buddhist story which admirably reflects the idea of the formative power of *karma*. This story comes from the *Saṃyutta Nikāya*.

One day the Buddha was at the Jetavana monastery in Sāvatthi when a Kosalan king named Pasenadi came to visit him. It was an unusual time of day for a visit and after the king was comfortably seated Gautama asked him why he was abroad at such an hour. The king unfolded a curious story. He had just come from the home of an important local official (the treasurer of Sāvatthi) who, having recently died without heir, had left a very considerable fortune to be gathered into the royal treasury. The deceased had owned ten million pieces of gold, and more silver than could be counted. Yet he had always eaten the worst and cheapest food, dressed in hempen rags, and traveled in a decrepit chariot. Why would so rich a man use such miserable things? The Buddha was ready with a reply:

> Formerly, great king, that householder and treasurer gave food in alms to a Private Buddha named Tagarasikkhi. But after he had given the order, saying "Give food to this monk," and had risen from his seat and departed, he repented him of the gift and said to himself, "It would have been better if my slaves or my servants had had this food." And, moreover, he murdered his brother's only son for the sake of the inheritance. Now whereas, great king, that householder and treasurer gave food in alms to the Private Buddha Tagarasikkhi, as the fruit of this deed he was born seven times in a higher state of existence, into a heavenly world; and as a further result of this deed he has held the treasurership seven times here in Sāvatthi. And whereas, great king, that householder and treasurer repented him of the gift, and said to himself, "It would have been better if my slaves or my servants had had this food," as a result of this sinful thought his mind has been averse to sumptuous food, to sumptuous clothing, to sumptuous equipages, to a sumptuous gratification of the five senses. And whereas, great king, the treasurer murdered his brother's only son for the sake of the inheritance, as a result of this deed he has suffered in hell for many years, for many hundreds of years, for many thousands of years, for many hundreds of thousands of years; and as a further result of this deed he has now for the seventh time died without leaving any son and forfeited his property into the royal treasury.[4]

As we have said, Gautama's use of the older Indian idea of *karma* led him eventually to a more comprehensive theory of causation in regard to human life, a theory of which *karma* became only one element, albeit an extremely important one. This wider theory is known by several names, among which are "the causal chain," "the chain of dependent origination," and the name we shall generally use, "conditioned co-production."

Conditioned Co-Production

The understanding of conditioned co-production is said, in the scriptures, to be a truth seen intuitively by the Buddha in his experience of enlightenment. No doubt we need not quibble about this, but the formulation of what was intuitively seen must have required some time, and it is unlikely that the versions known to us now are entirely free from the contributions of later systematicians, although strenuous subsequent efforts to make the theory as it stands more logical and coherent argue that at an early stage it was regarded as so much the Master's that it was better to interpret it than to improve it.

Gautama was concerned about the unsatisfactory nature of our life and preeminently about those elements which made it frustrating and unfulfilled. Chief among these, of course, is death, and next to it senility. What, he asked, are the causes of these calamities, or the factors in existence which make them possible? It suddenly occurred to Gautama while sitting under the Bodhi tree that the one absolutely essential condition of death is . . . birth! If we were not born, we would never suffer decay and death or any of the other "natural shocks that flesh is heir to." Very well, but what, then, is the necessary condition of birth?

Drawing upon presuppositions familiar in the Indian intellectual environment, Gautama concluded that birth depends upon the process of becoming (*bhava*). We are

born because a stream of becoming bears us along from
one life to another, with all the consequences of our actions and volitions being worked out. But on what does
becoming-existence depend?

The process of existence is continued because of the
power generated by our clinging to things, including existence itself. We attach ourselves to a million imagined
values and in our fear of nothingness we cling desperately
to life. Without such clinging the entire process of becoming would wind down. But why do we cling so desperately?

Thirst, that is, craving or desire (the familiar word in
Sanskrit is *trishnā;* in Pali, it is *tanhā*), is the cause upon
which our clinging depends. If we did not thirst for life,
we would not cling to it so tenaciously and, incidentally,
rob it by our very clinging of the relaxed charm it otherwise might have.

But thirst is not entirely self-generating. It is dependent
upon feeling (*vedanā*), for if we did not experience
pleasant and unpleasant feelings, we would remain indifferent to all that we encountered and thirst would not
arise.

Feeling, however, comes to be because of sensation. If
we were utterly without sensory experiences, no response
of feeling would be forthcoming. Remember that *manas,*
"mind" or "imagination," is numbered among the organs
of sense here, so that sensory deprivation, for a Buddhist,
would have to include the non-functioning of thought.
Clearly sense experience itself depends upon the contact
between sense organ and sense object, so here is one more
link in our causal chain. Nor can we stop here, for there is
a precondition for the encounter of organ and object: the
existence of our entire physical and psychological organism (*nāmarūpa,* literally "name-form"). We should note

in passing that since, in most Buddhist analyses, the connection between *nāmarūpa* and the six sense fields is so intimate that they are regarded as virtually synonymous, this particular step in the ladder of dependencies is sometimes omitted.

Are psyche and body, then, the root of the entire tree of suffering? By no means, for they too are dependent—upon consciousness! This certainly sounds strange to Western ears. By "consciousness" Gautama meant (at least for the present context) the sentient spark which, being ready for a birth, causes an embryo to come into being for its occupancy or as its expression. The assumption is that births are not fortuitous (whether parenthood is "planned" or not), but that minds and bodies are called into being—their *skandhas* gathered and assembled, as it were—in response to the need of consciousness or sentience which is an element within the stream of karmic becoming. It is hard, of course, to make such a notion plausible to modern, scientifically educated people (Eastern or Western), but the idea that "spirit" precedes body is not uncommon in the history of the world's cultures, and we have here the Theravāda version. It is the karmic stream which, bearing "consciousness," calls forth, as a vehicle for that consciousness, mind and psyche.

Even here we are not at the first cause of all our troubles, for consciousness itself has a cause. It arises because of the legacy of unexpended *karma* (in the form of predispositions shaped karmically by our history of volition, the technical name for these predispositions being *saṃskāra*). *Saṃskāra* is ontologically and causatively prior even to consciousness.

Yet *karma*, and the predispositions it governs, are themselves dependent. *Karma* is enabled to function only because men are ignorant of the great truths of Buddhism and in their ignorance act blindly. Here, at last, is the root of the tree. Let ignorance be destroyed and the tree will fall.

In reasoning thus, the Buddha was trying to achieve several objectives. He wished, obviously, to uncover the origin of all the defeating negations in life, the supreme of which is not exactly death, considered as a single incident, but death as the repeated symbol of transience and insubstantiality in every life sequence. But Gautama also intended to demonstrate that the inadequacy of human life cannot be overcome by all the meaningless quests which we quixotically undertake. Not wealth or power or prestige can save us from futility, for the king is ontologically as futile as the beggar. Ignorance is the base that has to be removed, and thirst or craving for existence and existing things is one of its foremost allies. In fact it is sometimes said that these two, ignorance and thirst, are really different manifestations of the same thing. Men live in illusion: the intellectual manifestation of that illusion is ignorance, the emotional is thirst.

More than this, however, Gautama has tried to show a mechanism whereby life continues even through death itself without there being any enduring self to support it. It is a process that runs on and is at every moment gathering to itself entirely fresh *dharmas;* there is no substance which floats along on the karmic flood, but the stream continues indefinitely.

The steps in the causal chain which we have outlined above are twelve in number, and for the sake of clarity, as well as to conform to the usual practice, we shall list them briefly:

1. Ignorance (Skt.: *avidyā;* Pali: *avijjā*)
2. Predispositions (Skt.: *saṃskāra;* Pali: *sankhāra*)
3. Consciousness (Skt.: *vijñāna;* Pali: *viññāna*)
4. Psyche and Body (Skt. and Pali: *nāmarūpa*)
5. The six senses (Skt. and Pali: *āyatana*)
6. Sensual contact (Skt.: *sparsha;* Pali: *phassa*)
7. Feeling (Skt. and Pali: *vedanā*)
8. Desire (Skt.: *trishnā;* Pali: *tanhā*)
9. Clinging (Skt. and Pali: *upādāna*)
10. Becoming-existence (Skt. and Pali: *bhava*)
11. Birth (Skt. and Pali: *jāti*)
12. Age, disease, death (Skt. and Pali: *jarāmarana*)

Here, then, are the phases in the human process. As you read this you are a point in the flowing turbulence, a sort of emergent occasion the dharmic transience of which is such that having now read an additional line or two you are a new structure. Since life, whatever its passing joys, is forever haunted and blighted by age, disease, and death, the man who has had enough of these and wishes to overcome them must begin his attack at the appropriate place. One cannot be satisfied with trimming the tree, even if that were possible. It is the whole thing, roots and all, that must fall. At this point an interesting, and possibly minor, difference between Theravāda and Mahāyāna is worth noting. The Theravādins in general have directed their attack upon thirst, or desire, feeling that if this is eradicated by disciplines of mind and body, enlightenment will ensue and ignorance will be abolished. The Mahāyānists, on the other hand, have usually made ignorance their primary target (although not without attendant assaults on passion) feeling that if the Truth is once seen, misplaced desire is instantly quelled. Both, however, have the aim of dissolving the causal factors entirely in order that the karmic process may reach an end.

In what has so far been said there has been implicit sometimes the concept of rebirth or transmigration. If death were really the end of the road for a particular stream of conscious becoming, one might as well eat, drink, and be as merry as possible for as long as possible or, if suffering made pleasure unattainable, one might his own quietus make with (or without) a bare bodkin. But death is, for Theravāda, not a terminal disease. What, then, is it? And what is meant by "transmigration"? There are some difficulties involved in these subjects which deserve careful scrutiny.

Death and Transmigration

> In Buddhism, death is nothing but living in a new environment. Whenever an existence disintegrates, the *kamma* by virtue of which it has been "burning" takes hold anew in a new location, and there sets alight a new I-process that unfolds itself into a new personality which is neither the same as the old one nor yet another but is a continuance from which both absolute diversity and absolute identity are excluded.[5]

Here is a bold statement of the essence of Theravāda teaching about death and its inevitable aftermath. Lest we think we are dealing here with the kind of reincarnational theory more common in other Indian systems or in some primitive cultures, the same authority adds:

> I take rise in my parents only in the same sense as the fountain takes its rise in the hill. Heirs of deeds, the Buddha calls living beings, not heirs of father and mother. They

spring from the womb of *kamma.* At every moment of my
existence I am the final member of a beginningless series
in a self-sustaining process.[6]

No soul or ego is to be found here reincarnated in a
series of bodies, so transmigration becomes merely a con-
tinuance of the series of mutually dependent but discrete
moments which is the karmic process. This is transmigration with no migrant. Another modern Theravādin explains
it thus:

> All of a man's good and bad acts leave behind their im-
> pressions in his mind; the accumulation of these impres-
> sions develops the tendencies and temperament of his
> personality. This process continues for the whole span of
> his life. At the moment of his death he falls into a sort of
> swoon in which this whole process of personality forma-
> tion is summed up. At his death the process of his con-
> sciousness flows on into another life on a plane correspond-
> ing to the level of mental development in his past life.
>
> Thus, for instance, the man whose actions have been
> bestial and irrational will get animal tendencies and tem-
> perament and will be reborn as an animal.[7]

One must not imagine that the concept of transmigration being discussed here is identical with that known to
the ancient Greeks. To be sure, one can find in Plato and
elsewhere references and inferences that may superficially
seem to be the Theravāda idea in a Hellenistic costume,
but there is at least one important difference. Platonic
views about death and reincarnation, inspired by Orphic
mysteries and, through them, by the Dionysian religion
of Thrace may have originated in Asia Minor or even
beyond and thus have known Indian, even Buddhist, influence; but they entailed metempsychosis—the idea that
continuity is established through an enduring soul or

psyche—whereas the Buddhist transmigrational theory is really better described perhaps as metasomatosis since continuity in the series is one of a sequence of material elements (*dharmas*) and is not borne by a soul. Even this is a dubious classification for Theravāda, however, since the continuity of the *dharma* series is really carried by the karmically consequential stream which is immaterial and impersonal.

Now, there is no doubt that the theory we have outlined presents certain difficulties. If life is a karmic series in which death is an incident no more significant than any other, and there is no soul or ego which holds the series together, what (we may well ask) can be charged by the Buddha with the responsibility of attaining *Nirvāna?* How can a collection of impersonal *dharmas* at one specific moment be effective in dealing with karmic consequences resulting from an action performed by an entirely different set of *dharmas* at another time? Surely continuity is essential to any idea of working progressively for enlightenment or salvation, yet where is there room for, or ground for, continuity here? Is not the human being, in Theravāda Buddhism, rather like an ax? A man might foolishly say, "I've had this ax for twenty years; of course, it's had ten new heads and eighteen handles, but it's the same old ax!" We would laugh at such a statement, but is there anything less absurd about Theravādin continuity without a continuing entity? One might even speculate that the primary usefulness of the Greek notion of soul was precisely to overcome the problem we seem to encounter here by providing the ground for meaningful and effective continuity. The Hebrew-Christian tradition (until the latter borrowed the Hellenistic soul concept) managed to find ground for continuity in the idea that all sentient life was sustained by God in whom we live and move and have our being. But how shall Theravāda accomplish its end lacking both a soul and a God?

Western critics have been particularly severe at this point. The usually sympathetic Winston King remarks:

> There is a difficulty here, to be sure, which is evaded as the rule. The factors of permanence, unity and seeming identity are unexplained or under-valued. And the peculiar unity-in-change which is characteristic of mental life is almost completely denied in theory, but accepted in fact. That is: the kammic impulse which goes from life to life is theoretically not a soul or self; but it contains implicitly or potentially moral and mental character, memory and full self-identification with the past lives. This is a marvellous kind of "mere energy" which can carry the memory of a million lives and their moral quality through rebirths as ghosts in hells, animal, god and man of many sorts! [8]

Another critic observes that the Platonic concept of reincarnation was more logical than the Theravādin and points out that the non-ego idea makes it very hard to see how a Buddha could meaningfully identify himself with someone who lived many thousands of years ago and began then the career which has finally resulted in Buddhahood.[9]

It would be foolish to assume that no one saw a difficulty in the Buddha's anātman-transmigration teaching until Westerners began to take an interest, and a study of the Pali scriptures indicates that Gautama had, in fact, to defend the doctrine against misunderstanding and charges of irrationality during his own lifetime. How did he deal with his assailants?

Above all, Gautama's concern was to prevent his critics from mitigating the purity of his idea, even though by doing so they might have found it easier to accept what he said. Thus, in the *Majjhima Nikāya* we find a man named Sati arguing that Gautama must really mean that consciousness (*vijñāna*) is the enduring link between lives in the same sequence, and to this Gautama patiently explains the now familiar doctrine that each of the sensory consciousnesses is dependent upon the sense experience to which it relates, so that without sense experience there can be no consciousness. It follows, then, that consciousness, being dependent for its origin, can hardly be the substratum or cause of everything else in our life. Yet Gautama repeatedly refuses to endorse the apparent logical consequence of this, that death is the termination of a stream of conscious becoming. There is, in the Buddha's thought, no denial of the reality of our process-existence, no denial of the reality of our actions, yet there is the emphatic denial of any enduring *entity*.

A. B. Keith, who, although an excellent scholar, fluctuated between patronizing and condemning many aspects of Buddhist thought, tried to make Gautama's view more rational by arguing that Sati's problem was not that he wanted consciousness to persist through all changes, including death, but that he wanted it to do so without itself undergoing change. And Keith thinks that there is at least one scriptural passage in which we are given a clue to the truth. He reminds us that in the *Saṃyutta Nikāya* there is a story about Godhika, a very advanced adept in Buddhism, who committed suicide because disease made maintenance of trance impossible. Knowing his intention, Mara, the Evil One, hovered in the form of smoke, seeking to catch the rebirth-consciousness of the sage. He could not find it, however, because it had vanished with the attainment of *Nirvāna*. Now, Keith says, we have in this an important hint. Must we not assume that Mara is experienced in his business and by no means a fool? There must, therefore, have been some point to his watching for the rebirth-consciousness. The only reason for his not finding it, then, must have been Godhika's attainment of *Nirvāna*, and the Buddha's teaching must mean that consciousness does indeed form the continuing link between moments and lives, but that while persisting, it undergoes change of some sort. Only with *Nirvāna* does consciousness itself cease entirely to function.

Keith's explanation is ingenious and, I think, essentially correct. Yet as it stands the interpretation Keith gives us, especially if it is pressed in too naïve or literal a fashion, probably amounts to eisegesis, putting more into the text than can safely be drawn out of it. The Buddha was perfectly aware that memory exists and that we have a sense of continuity; but to make consciousness the bridge between moments and existences seems to instate it as a soul under a new name.

Indeed the Buddha was usually far more concerned to guide his questioners away from what he regarded as dangerous error than to specify precisely the truth about transmigration, and we are left with a formula that will always raise questions for the philosopher. What is offered to us is a theory of potentially endless transmigration: of a continuum without a continuant—or, rather, a continuant that must be thought of under the category of quality rather than substance or spirit. Karmic character continues, but there is no person who owns the character. If this is unsatisfactory and we wish to press the Buddha to be more explicit, we may be embarrassed to find ourselves occupying the place of a questioner who once asked:

So then you say that body is not the Self; feeling is not the
Self; likewise perception, the activities and consciousness.
Then what self can those acts affect which are not self-
wrought?

To this the Buddha, displaying the caustic sternness of
the Oriental master, replied:

It is possible, brethren, that some senseless fellow, sunk
in ignorance and led astray by craving, may think to go
beyond the Master's teaching thus: "So then you say that
body is not the Self; that feeling is not the Self; that perception, the activities . . . consciousness is not the Self.
Then what self can those acts affect which are not self-
wrought?" [10]

Those of us who prefer not to be publicly castigated as
senseless fellows must, presumably, be content to know
that all is *anicca* (Pali)—insubstantial and impermanent
—yet there is a life continuum in which death is merely an
incident and dissatisfaction is endemic. To escape this is
our task, and our goal is *Nirvāna*.

Nirvāna

We have already examined the idea of *Nirvāna* in Theravāda, and little needs to be added now, as we think of it
as the culmination of successful endeavor in personal
existence. *Nirvāna* literally means "extinction" and points
to the "blowing out" of the fires of lust and clinging which
force us to go through the cycle of rebirths. To attain
Nirvāna is to know, even while we still live out the dregs
of a karmically conditioned physical existence, that no rebirth will ever overtake us. It is to experience freedom
and peace—or, rather, a state beyond anything those

words normally suggest. *Nirvāna* is unconditioned and, therefore, eternally beyond change and decay yet (being a *dharma*, as our classification in Chapter IV indicated) it is without self or ego. It does not, therefore, constitute the permanent endurance of our individualities and, indeed, it cannot be known until we have learned to forsake the longing for this.

When a man who has attained *Nirvāna* dies he is said to have entered *Parinirvāna* which means *Nirvāna* beyond all the reaches of karmic or material reality. This is to be utterly delivered from all anguish, all pain, all the unsatisfying experiences which fill our sentient days. But it does not mean a simple annihilation. Beyond the specifying of what *Parinirvāna* does *not* mean we cannot really go, for only he who has reached it knows; its lineaments cannot be defined by thought since it forever transcends all experience except the experience of itself.

MAHĀYĀNA

Theravāda, as we have seen, pictured a man as a collection of *dharmas* which spuriously produced the illusion of enduring selfhood. Mahāyāna, having driven its analysis to the point of abandoning the substantiality of even the *dharmas*, and having discovered *Śūnyatā*, the Absolute *Dharma* that is simultaneously each reality and all Reality, had to recast its understanding of man accordingly. Indeed, everything that concerns our human existence—*karma*, ignorance, causation, death, transmigration, and all else—now acquires a new perspective and some altered implications.

Perhaps we shall most clearly see the Mahāyāna deviation[11] if we begin with the prongs of the fork on which

we are all existentially impaled: ignorance and desire.
Let us start with desire. This was, from a very early time,
an element in the chain or ladder of dependent co-production, but it had a special status there inasmuch as it was a
prime target of Buddhist discipline. Desire arose because
the human organism experienced desirable feelings as a
result of its sensory contact with the passing world, and
immensely popular techniques for frustrating desire by
convincing oneself that the world was, after all, not desirable became important parts of Buddhist life (thus one
was enjoined to contemplate corpses in various stages of
decay, for instance, to dispel any attachment one might
feel to the body).

With Mahāyāna came a new approach which saw a
serious weakness in the older preoccupation with the
elimination of desire. One problem faced by those who
would eliminate craving is the strength and status of the
foe. With *karma* it is a fundamental force in the world of
constant becoming. In fact, from certain perspectives it
might be said that it is desire that makes the world go
round. D. T. Suzuki boldly writes: *"Trishnā* wants to see,
and we have eyes; it wants to hear, and we have ears; it
wants to jump and we have the deer, the rabbit and other
animals of this order; it wants to fly and we have birds of
all kinds." He even affirms: *"Trishnā* lies in us not as one
of the factors constituting our consciousness, but it is our
being itself. It is I; it is you; it is the cat; it is the tree; it is
the rock; it is the snow; it is the atom." [12]

No doubt one should allow for understandable hyper-
bole as Suzuki strains to make his point, but his point is
important. Without the force of desire we would not have
come to be, according to Buddhism, and an assault on it
is therefore an ambiguous operation, for even if all other

forms of craving are conquered, we shall be left with the
desire to be desireless! Shall we, then, ever reach genuine
freedom from *trishnā?* Perhaps, but it is obviously a
strenuous program that leads to that felicitous end.

Furthermore, to mount an assault on desire may involve
us in serious error, for it may involve an objectifying of
trishnā in our thinking which sets it over against us and
thus creates in our imagination a new facet of that pervasive dualism which is the first product of our chronic
ignorance. Here we arrive at the other prong of the fork
on which we writhe, and the Mahāyānist, although by no
means repudiating the need to attack *trishnā* by various
disciplines, conceived that the main thrust of our attack
should be against dualistic ignorance, for here is the error
the elimination of which will overcome even craving.

The problem of our ignorance and its propensity for
dividing reality into dual entities (subject-object, me–not
me, truth-error, good-evil, and so on) is illustrated by a
curious incident recounted by the great Chinese Ch'an
(Zen) patriarch Hui Neng in his *Platform Sūtra.*[13] Hung
Jen, celebrated by Zen as the fifth patriarch of that sect,
and Hui Neng's master, one day sought to discover among
his disciples a suitable successor. He invited them to submit a stanza expressing the Truth and declared that whoever best performed this task would become the sixth
patriarch. Most of the disciples were convinced that the
winner would be a man named Shen Hsiu and, in fact,
declined to bother competing. Shen Hsiu wrote a verse
that may be paraphrased as follows:

> The body is a tree of enlightenment,
> And Mind a shining mirror.
> Wipe the mirror constantly
> To keep it free of dust.

Upon reading this, Hui Neng was dissatisfied and wrote a stanza of his own:

> Enlightenment has no tree
> And no reflecting mirror.
> Since the Void is all
> What *dust* could obscure *what?*

It was Hui Neng's verse that pleased Hung Jen, although his acceptance of it was kept secret for fear that the relatively unknown Hui Neng would be attacked and injured by jealous rivals. What makes his verse superior, by Buddhist standards? The answer is simple: it accurately accuses Shen Hsiu's poem of being dualistic—in fact of falling into the very error that Mahāyāna sees as the root of our intellectual dilemma. Our mind (the "mirror") and error ("dust") are separated as if each were finally real, but the Truth that is all Reality is *not* dual. To know this is to know the futility of wiping dust from the mind-mirror, for there is no legitimate distinction to be made in *Śūnyatā* between the reality of the dust and the reality of the mirror—there is but one Reality!

To know the Truth, then, is to know that the Real can desire nothing, for there is nothing it is not, nothing it lacks—*and I am the Real!* Thus the ground of desire is cut away as the ignorance that beclouds us is overcome.

To be a little more precise, the ignorance out of which all our sufferings come has two chief facets. The first is our failure to understand that our true nature is the Buddha-Nature, the Absolute. The second is our failure to see that the same Buddha-Nature is the nature of all beings, and in being so is not in the least divided. Lacking this knowledge (and especially lacking it as an intuitive experience of non-separation), we become vulnerable to im-

pulses and desires of many kinds; wanting, straining toward, acquiring things, and dominating persons. The
futility of this is no longer simply, as in Theravāda, the
consequence of the transience and composite character of
things but of the fact that there is no essential gulf between desirer and desired. He who desires, the object
of desire, and the relationship between them are all
Śūnyatā. There can be, in Truth, no other.

But now an inevitable question intrudes itself: What is
the seat of ignorance and error? And, beyond this, how do
they arise? We have glanced at these problems in another
context, but it may be useful to look at them again.

Obviously it is not enough to say that *I* am the ground
or seat of ignorance, for that would impute too much
"reality" to my individuality. It can only be *Śūnyatā* itself
that is the final locus of error and illusion. More than that,
if illusion exists, *its* reality must actually *be Śūnyatā*. Yet
how is this thinkable? And if it is the case, how can we
hope for deliverance? Can we imagine the arising of ignorance as the self-expression of the Absolute?

D. T. Suzuki writes: "As to the question how and why
this negative principle of ignorance came to assert itself
in the body of Suchness, we are at a loss where to find an
authoritative and definite answer to it." [14] Suzuki shifts the
field of discussion from philosophy to psychology, offering
only two suggestions, of questionable use to us. One of
these is that ignorance is "inherent in Suchness, though
only hypothetically, illusively, apparently, and not really
in any sense." [15] But what can the illusion or mere appearance of ignorance mean when ignorance is so mon-
umental a human problem? The illusion of an illusion is
still an illusion. Suzuki's second contribution is the re-
minder that Aśvaghosha defined ignorance as "a spark of

consciousness that spontaneously flashes from the unfathomable depths of Suchness." [16] Precisely. But how? And why?

It is clear that none of this answers our questions, but it may be the best that can be done. The overcoming of ignorance and the climbing of Mount Everest challenge us for much the same reason: ignorance and Everest are there! Ontologically inexplicable, ignorance is a fact and as *Śūnyatā* is the Truth it must also be the Ignorance. If this raises questions about the status of the struggle we face to overcome ignorance, the questions simply cannot be adequately answered. But the questions are only relevant, presumably, until the ignorance is overcome; when it is overcome the questions have vanished with the ignorance. Or have they? In any case it is important to note that when Mahāyāna became an absolutism, the problem of human ignorance became radically changed. No longer a quality of a stream of dharmic multiplicity, it is inseparable from the Absolute, the Truth itself. Truth and illusion are one. This, of course, makes no logical sense, but that may be the fault of logic.

Karma

In what ways does Mahāyāna's *Śūnyatā* doctrine affect the concept of *karma?* Here again we can detect significant changes of perspective.

Karma remains, for Mahāyāna, a force that carries the world along so long as egoistic action persists. It shapes us in perfectly recognizable ways: "We do, and our 'doing' inevitably makes its influence felt on our way of feeling, sensing and thinking. . . . Our way of feeling, sensing and thinking thus influenced then inevitably conditions the further steps of our doing." [17] But the reach of *karma* is much wider than this, and it is better not to think of it individualistically at all, since we are not separate essences, but all of us are bound together in that chain of mutuality and even oneness that is the Buddha-Nature. *Karma* is therefore a universal rather than a personal or individual thing. Deeds establish or perpetuate a chain of consequences that affects, however minutely, the entire fabric of existence, rather as a dropped pebble sends waves across the entire surface of a pond. The whole universe (*Dharmadhātu*) is touched by every willed event.

In search of clarity let us personalize what we have been saying. I am *Śūnyatā*. Consequently I discover in my Self the experience of *all* sentient beings—every sinner and every saint, every brutish mind and every poet, every violent man and every victim—all, in a sense, live in me at every moment. So I am not just the bearer of my own particular *karma*, but in affirming myself as Absolute, I declare myself to be the true bearer of all. To understand this is to learn patient acceptance, for if I suffer as the victim of cruelty, I am also the perpetrator of the outrage and at that level of awareness where my proud little ego is abandoned, I surmount the trials of both. If I suffer misfortune today, it is not necessarily because I—or a continuity which the pronoun "I" specifies—performed an action of which this is the karmic outcome, but because evil has been done and that evil breeds somewhere its inevitable effect. The true and deepest bearer of *karma* is not the individual but the Void—the Reality of all individuals.

In Indian thought generally *karma* has been considered a highly deterministic thing. Where the emphasis fell upon *karma* as a past phenomenon its power to shape our

present has been of supreme interest and sometimes this
has led to a sense of resignation to whatever a man found
to be his lot. In Buddhism, however, and especially in
Japan, the emphasis tends to be on the *future* consequences of *karma* and on our responsibility so to act and
respond to circumstances that our future—and the future
in general—enjoys improvement. It remains true, of
course, that the past shapes my present, but since *Śūnyatā*
is All in a temporal as well as in an ontological sense, the
entire past is gathered in every moment, for every moment
is eternity. Thus there is a sense in which nothing outside
the present moment really determines me. I am, consequently, totally responsible for my life and I am determined by nothing outside my true Self. To escape the
determinism of *karma*, therefore, I must escape the bind-
ing illusion of my individual self's finality and discover
the ultimate Self in which *karma* is transcended. As an individual I am borne along on the river of *karma*, but as the
Śūnyatā-Self I bear *karma* and am consequently free.

We may see, then, that as in everything else Mahāyāna's
concept of *karma* is a centrifugal circling around the
pivotal idea of the Void. It acquires a different flavor from
that tasted in Theravāda's analysis.

Death and Transmigration

The events of death and transmigration have always
been tied closely, in India, to the belief in *karma*. In what
way, then, are these affected by an absolutism of the Buddhist kind?

It is customary among men to regard death as the
antithesis of life. Among the Stoics it was said that these
two could never meet, for while life was present death

was not, and when death arrived life was gone. Such a dualism could hardly be tolerated in Mahāyāna. Here all apparent polarities and antitheses are brought together in the concept of the indivisible Suchness which is both unborn and undying. It follows, then, that we must not think of ourselves as living until we die, but we must see that life and death are not actually separate realities. The moment life begins in a baby, death begins too and both proceed together. Indeed, it is only because under the illusion of individual and independent identity we rationalize and objectify both life and death that we set them apart. Masao Abe likens life and death to the two sides of the same sheet of paper: the paper is simultaneously and at all times both.[18] All that is mundane is temporary, but the true Suchness of all that is is beyond the very categories of life and death in its essence and *is* both life and death insofar as these have any actuality at all.

To realize our Suchness, then, is at the same time to know what Zen is fond of calling the "Great Death" which is the termination of our clinging to all that passes and the end of our illusion that our finite being is a valuable island to be protected at all costs from the encroachments of the surrounding terrible sea of non-being. And to realize all this is to know the manifestation of "Great Life"—the life of the never born, never dying, Reality. Death and life are, thus, swallowed up in *Śūnyatā* which bears them but is unmarked by them.

Nor can the idea of transmigration remain unaffected by the affirmation of the Void. It is true, of course, that many Mahāyānists retain quite a literal acceptance of scriptural references to heavens, hells, and reincarnation, but for Mahāyāna philosophers this has increasingly become difficult to maintain. Instead, the tendency has been to think

of transmigration no longer horizontally (a process run-
ning from past through present to future in some individual stream of life) but vertically. If all that is can be
thought of as the manifestation of *Śūnyatā* or of the
Dharma Mind, then the person who I am at this moment
may certainly identify himself with *any* past life as well
as with all present and future lives. That which is my
Reality was also that of the Buddha and of all those lives
traced in the Jataka Tales as the preliminary existences of
Gautama. It is as true for me to say that I was once Gautama as to say that I am now Douglas Fox, not because
some elusive spirit has been repeatedly embodied, nor
because a continuity of karmic consequences has kept a
particular line of dharmic becoming alive, but because all
that has ever appeared and all that shall appear owns the
same Suchness.

Here we must beware of a common error. What I have
just said may sound as though *Śūnyatā* is, after all, merely
a reversion to the older Indian idea of Brahman, the One
who alone truly is. In many respects *Śūnyatā* and Brahman
are alike, but Buddhists insist that they are not identical
ideas. If one holds the typical Vedāntic *Brahman-Ātman*
doctrine, the world and all that it contains are reduced to
the status of *maya*—the creative but illusory display of
divine power—so that it can fairly be said that when one
realizes his *Ātman*-consciousness the world disappears. In
Buddhism, on the other hand, care is taken to avoid class-
ifying the world in any way that might suggest that it is
merely illusion. The true illusion, for a Buddhist who
retains his Mādhyamikan heritage, lies in our misinterpret-
ing the facts of the world; in our imputing substance and
aseity where there is none. The world is not "unreal" but
our way of viewing it ordinarily is mistaken. Each instance

of existence is "real" inasmuch as its Suchness is *Śūnyatā*, and for this reason we may find the Truth, in Buddhist opinion, not by escaping the world but by seeing it properly. Thus a man may awaken to the Truth when he is grasped by the startling mystery of a snowflake; a flower may become my window to Reality; the Truth lives not apart from the world but *as* the world—but never as the unenlightened man sees the world.

It must be acknowledged, however, that as Yogācāra speculation idealized the *Śūnyatā* idea, its similarity to the Brahman concept became more acute. An idealistic Buddhist might sound very much like a Vedāntist when he says that worldly entities are like ideas the *Ālayavijñāna* creatively produces and are real only as ideas are real.

Thus we arrive at the point where we can begin to understand Mahāyāna teaching about *Nirvāna*, a teaching at once simple and profound.

Nirvāna

Nirvāna is not a place; it is not even a "state of mind"; it is by no means a refuge from the world. Rather, *Nirvāna* is the perfect fulfillment of every sentient being, for it is his return to an understanding of the Truth. More than that, it is his realization that he *is* the Truth and that the world about him is no less so. *Samsāra*—the world of transience and rebirth—is *Nirvāna*. They are not antitheses any more than are life and death, for to see either truly is to see Suchness itself. *Nirvāna* seen through the discriminating and dualizing eyes of our clouded existential life is *samsāra: samsāra* seen through the joyous eyes of awakening is *Nirvāna*. Herein lies the strange power of many simple Japanese haiku in which the poet, speaking of the plainest of things, suggests that in them and not apart from them the ultimate Truth lies. If we have eyes to see, we know that Basho was celebrating Infinity when he wrote:

> Ah! the first, the gentlest fall of snow;
> Enough to make the jonquil-leaves bend low.

VI

THE WAY AND THE WAYFARERS

THERAVĀDA

In Theravāda Buddhism the way of escape from ignorance and craving is emphatically one of self-help. There is no God to offer us grace, no savior to join with us in the struggle, no saints whose merit can be diverted to our deliverance. We are on our own. In the Pali tradition the last recorded words of the Buddha were: "Work out your salvation with diligence," a sentence verbally like but fundamentally different from the New Testament's advice: "You must work out your own salvation in fear and trembling; for it is God who works in you, inspiring both the will and the deed." [1] In Theravāda there are ample grounds for the earnestness that is signified by the Biblical phrase "fear and trembling," but there is no divine spirit working in us and for us and with us. The *Dhammapada* sums up the situation with admirable clarity and precision:

> By oneself the evil is done, by oneself one is defiled. Purity and impurity belong to oneself, no one can purify another. Let no one forget his own good for the sake of another's, however great.[2]

Here is a radical individualism, yet we must remember

145

that it is a practical rather than a philosophical individualism, for in truth there is no "self" which might endure to
undo the evil it has done. To discuss the way of enlightenment, we must constantly speak as if we had forgotten all
that has been said about *anātman*, but this is because our
systems of language and of imperfect understanding leave
us no alternative. With all that we say in this chapter we
must hold our previous ideas in uncomfortable partnership.
Theravāda's Way to Truth may be approached from several directions. We may, for example, examine the attributes that a Buddhist is expected to acquire as he pro-
gresses, and certainly it is appropriate that we at least
consider the nature of that profoundly important "detachment," and the five cardinal Buddhist virtues which
Theravāda disciplines are expected to nourish. We shall,
however, after looking at these, make our approach by an
analysis of the so-called Threefold Discipline which was,
in effect, a methodological rephrasing of the Buddha's
Eightfold Path.

Detachment

For a Theravādin, everything is impermanent and without substance. Consequently nothing can be a solace for
men in their ill-fated quest for endurance, but all things
become merely additional grounds for frustration when
men cling to them with hope. When a man attains a complete understanding that existents are impermanent
(Pali: *anicca*), without ego (Skt.: *anātman;* Pali: *anattā*),
and therefore potential ingredients in his anguish (Pali:
dukkha), he is ready to learn detachment from them and to
proceed from there to a liberation from the bondage of
the cycle of birth and death.

Detachment must be both intellectual and emotional. To achieve it we must begin by seeing things as they are; by seeing objects and our own mental or emotional states without the usual interpretative overlay that imputes values and meanings to them. Our emotional states, for example, will then be seen as arising from certain causes, as consisting of certain feelings, and as being supplanted at last by other emotions. In all this we shall learn to regard emotion as an exceedingly transient phenomenon of no special importance and emphatically not as possessed by some persisting self. Introspection thus actually leads to the abandonment of the sense of "I." Similarly, external objects must be seen not as useful or attractive or even repellent (for this is to see them as possessing a value for an "I") but simply as they are in the most matter-of-fact fashion. A delightful illustration of this degree of detachment is to be found in the *Visuddhimagga* and concerns a very notable monk named Mahātissa:

> The story is that a certain woman had married into a family of rank, but had quarreled with her husband, and, decked and ornamented, until she looked like a goddess, had issued forth from Anurādhapura, early in the morning, and was returning home to her family. On her way she met the elder, as he was on his way from Mt. Cetiya to go on his begging-rounds in Anurādhapura. And no sooner had she seen him, than the perversity of her nature caused her to laugh loudly. The elder looked up inquiringly, and observing her teeth, realized the impurity of the body, and attained to saintship. . . . Then came her husband, following in her footsteps, and seeing the elder, he said: "Reverend sir, have you seen a woman pass this way?" And the elder said: "Whether it was a woman or a man who passed this way I cannot tell. But a set of bones is traveling along this road." [3]

To see a beautiful woman as a mass of transient *skandhas*, as already corroding matter, and, far from being attracted to her, to be delivered by the sight of her from any remaining attachment to the body is indeed to have progressed far along the Buddhist road. Beyond even this, however, one should at last achieve the ability to move amid the flux of things with no deliberate attention or inattention to them at all, to allow things to confront us without the entanglement of our interest. As Edward Conze observes in a sentence worthy of reflection, "a mind which sees, hears, etc., is a distracted, malfunctioning mind." [4] Here, too, Buddhaghosa's remarkable work, *Visuddhimagga*, provides an illustration: A monk named Cittaguta lived in a cave in which a splendid painting was hanging. One day a party of traveling monks visited him, eager to learn something from him since he was celebrated for his spiritual attainments. One of the younger monks, having explored the cave and found the painting, began to express amazed delight: "What a beautiful painting!" Cittaguta's response must, one imagines, have produced the sort of painful silence that every enthusiast eventually suffers, for he said: "For more than sixty years, brethren, I have lived in this cave, and I have never known whether there is a painting there or not. Today only have I learned it from you." [5]

The detachment which the Theravādin seeks must be so complete that it negates all our impulses toward ambition, personal hope, and acquisition. The man of detachment should live a life that purposes nothing, not even the attainment of *Nirvāna*, for to cling to the Absolute Truth itself with desire to attain it is still to be imprisoned in the spurious self's struggle to fulfill itself. Absolute release from our birth-death prison comes only with absolute detachment from all that the ego might think to acquire and possess. Obviously the attainment of this degree of disinterestedness is a matter of immeasurable difficulty, and it is no wonder that Theravādins have often thought of it as requiring a great number of lifetimes. Nor is it any wonder that the typical lay Theravādin accepts for his present life a more attainable goal—the improvement of his *karma* through meritorious actions.

Five Cardinal Virtues

The achievement of perfect detachment and consequent enlightenment is dependent upon the development of five "faculties" or virtues: faith, vigor, mindfulness, concentration, and wisdom. A brief, and not entirely limpid, explanation of these is given in the *Saṃyutta Nikāya:*

> And of what sort, monks, is the faculty of faith? Herein an Aryan disciple has faith: he has faith in the enlightenment of the Tathagata (Buddha). . . . And what is the faculty of vigor? It is the vigor that one lays hold of in practising the four right efforts. And what is the faculty of mindfulness? It is the mindfulness one lays hold of in practising the four applications of mindfulness. And what is the faculty of concentration? Herein the Aryan disciple, having made relinquishing the object of meditation, attains concentration, attains one-pointedness of mind. And what is the faculty of wisdom? Herein the Aryan disciple has wisdom: he is endowed with wisdom leading to the knowledge of rise and fall, Aryan, piercing, leading rightly to the extinction of suffering. This, monks, is called the faculty of wisdom.[6]

A further word of explanation, although it must be brief, will probably be welcome.

Faith is an important quality for the person who wishes to set out on the Buddhist pilgrimage, for the road can hardly be followed for a single step without it. Faith means confidence in and commitment to the Buddha as the one who brings life's highest truth to us, to the *sangha*, or Buddhist community, as the protector of that truth and nourisher of the faithful, and to the Truth (*Dharma*) itself as unfailingly effective in producing enlightenment. Faith in the Buddha would not be enough, for unless the *sangha* has reproduced the Buddha's teaching with fidelity we do not know what the Buddha has to offer. And faith in the reality of the Buddha's enlightenment similarly is useless unless we are confident that his teaching itself will enable us to reproduce in ourselves, sooner or later, a similar awakening. Thus faith involves a willingness to "bet one's life" on doctrines and disciplines before one has had enough experience to *know* that they are true or effective. Of course the Buddhist holds that our faith should progressively, and experientially, be supplanted by "knowledge" as we move toward enlightenment ourselves. Here, however, a problem arises for the philosopher.

Philosophy is a rational enterprise. It makes and examines statements with all the tools that human reason has or can devise for that purpose, but it limits itself to those tools. When, therefore, the Buddhist proclaims a "knowledge" that is immediate, intuitive, certain, and beyond all mere faith, the philosopher finds himself with two obligations: (1) he may use his philosophical tools to explicate and illuminate what the Buddhist experience is held to mean, clearly indicating the points at which this meaning goes beyond the province of philosophy itself. This is what we have been trying to do throughout this book. But (2) he must, in fidelity to his critical tools and methods, express skepticism about the epistemic reliability of the supra-rational experience the meaning of which he has been discussing.

Buddhist philosophy, therefore, is engaged in the attempt to explicate the meaning of the central generating experience of Buddhism, and in the course of doing so, it engages to make clear that this experience is felt by Buddhists to go beyond faith, but to require the venture of faith for its attainment. Having done this, the philosopher—Buddhist or otherwise, so long as he is really a philosopher—must raise the question of the authenticity of the "knowledge" presumed to be discovered in the generating experience. He must point out that such "knowledge" cannot be demonstrated to be actual knowledge by any criterion which the philosopher may recognize. Further, he must ask whether faith has really been transcended in this final enlightenment experience, or whether one is not, to the very end, in need of a faith-full conviction that the experience of enlightenment itself, for all its sense of direct and unquestionable "knowing," is really a meeting with Truth and not the most subtle of all illusions.

The religious person commits himself in faith. This the philosopher (who may himself be a religious person) understands. But the philosophical spirit *within* the religious person must, if it is not stricken dumb, continue to ask disquieting questions or faith becomes fanaticism and its alleged transcendence in direct knowledge the final pathetic act of self-deception.

The virtue of faith, therefore, must be recognized by

those of us who choose to be philosophers (whatever else
we also choose to be) as an attitude indispensable to the
eventual attainment of the generating experience of Buddhism, but partly superseded by that experience itself.
As philosophers we need not doubt that such faith is
known and that it leads, at times, to the experience sought.
But *as* philosophers we must continue to entertain reserva-
tions about the significance claimed for that experience.
This raises the question of whether a philosopher can advance very far in the Buddhist life without forsaking or
compromising his commitment to philosophy. I would
argue that this is an experimental question not to be set-
tled a priori. A faith is possible that contains its own
doubt, and it may be that an Absolute Knowledge is possible which fulfills philosophical skepticism—containing
it, as it were, without disturbance but also without compromise.

Vigor is a virtue which, happily, needs little explanation. In Buddhism it refers chiefly to the energy that a man
expends to make what are called the "four right efforts."
These efforts, incumbent upon all faithful Buddhists, are
(1) to avoid or prevent the arising of evil or unwholesome
dharmas; (2) to abandon and overcome such evil *dharmas*
as have already arisen; (3) to effect the arising of good
or wholesome *dharmas;* (4) to effect the maintenance and
increase of such good *dharmas* as already exist. In short,
the vigor that is a Buddhist virtue is that with which we
seek to promote the good and overcome evil.

Mindfulness means the awareness we must give to all
that occurs within or outside us which might produce
spiritual disturbance or promote self-centered illusion.
We become "mindful" of sense data when we refuse to let

it seduce us into attributing false meaning to it or into attaching spurious value to it, but see it exactly as it is— arising from that cause, enduring as that entity, decaying in that impermanence. Thoughts, emotions, physical sensations, and objective things or events must all be viewed "mindfully" in order that, having penetrated their true status, we may prevent them from disrupting the growing tranquillity of our detachment. Mindfulness is, then, the very antithesis of discursive thought or enthusiastic valuing.

Concentration is a more difficult virtue to perfect, or even to understand, for it refers to the exercise of "concentrating" our awareness by withdrawing it increasingly from external stimuli and from the typical rushing mass of disorganized ideas that inhabit our mind. Various techniques may be employed in this pursuit and it involves the successive mastery of the so-called "four trances" and "four formless attainments" which are the proper subject of a book on Buddhist methods rather than on Buddhist philosophy. Whereas our mind is usually a wasteful diffusion of mental effort, an undisciplined rushing after the winds, "concentration" is a centering of awareness that progressively rejects all sense impressions and all that is the fruit of such impressions until, all trivia being removed, only the Truth remains; and this is found to owe nothing to sense impressions or to the ordinary functions of imagination.

Wisdom, the last of these great virtues, is delusion-free Truth-seeing and is thus the culmination and perfection of the other virtues.

Already it may be seen that the Theravāda Way is exacting, and it is inevitable that men should want to have some way of measuring progress in it. To this end, Buddhists began to speak of stages of attainment and in the most common arrangement of these there are four:

Four Stages of Attainment

1. The Stream-Entrant (Pali: *Sotāpanna*): The person who has reached this stage is said to have already broken the first three of ten "fetters" which are said to bind us to our state of ignorance. These fetters are belief in a self, doubt about the Buddha or his teaching, and reliance in good works or ceremonies to deliver us from our existential problems.

2. The Once-Returner (Pali: *Sakadāgāmin*): Here is a person who has greatly reduced the power of two more fetters—lust and hate—and is so far advanced toward perfection that he may expect to be reborn into this world only once more.

3. The Non-Returner (Pali: *Anāgāmin*): He is now entirely liberated from the first five fetters and will not be reborn in our world. If he is born again, it will be in a special "Brahma world" and not in any mere terrestrial or heavenly realm.

4. The Worthy (Skt.: *Arhat;* Pali: *Arahat*): This person has destroyed the remaining five fetters (desire for life in the realm of form, desire for life in the formless realm, pride, restlessness, and ignorance). The *Arhat* is, thus, one who has completed the course set for him by Buddhism and has attained *Nirvāna*.

Threefold Discipline

The attainment of *Nirvāna* through the perfection of the virtues and of non-attachment to all that is transient or misleading requires enormous effort, and to understand this we should now consider the Theravāda Way from a different point of view: the elaboration of the so-called Threefold Discipline. This represents a reformulation of the elements in the Eightfold Path as taught by Gautama and it is thus an attempt to specify the developmental tasks of Buddhism—the skills that must be mastered and the qualities perfected before the highest enlightenment can be known. It must not be thought of as displacing the older Eightfold Path but merely as reformulating it in a way found more congenial by many Buddhists.

The elements of the Threefold Discipline are Morality (Skt. and Pali: *Sīla*), Concentration, or Meditation (Skt. and Pali: *Samādhi*), and Wisdom (Skt.: *Prajñā;* Pali: *Paññā*). We must examine each in turn.

Sīla

Sīla means literally "habitual behavior" or even "character," but in the present context it signifies the practical moral norms of Theravāda. As a formal category within the range of Buddhist disciplines it embraces three of the phases in the Eightfold Path: Right Speech, Right Action, and Right Livelihood.

When a man decides to set out on the Theravāda Way, his first step should be to make an affirmation of his faith and to accept responsibility for living according to a basic and minimal set of moral rules. His faith is affirmed by the declaration that he takes "refuge" in the Buddha, the *dharma,* and the *sangha,* and the minimal norms of Buddhism are taught as five simple but far-reaching precepts: (1) to abstain from taking life; (2) to abstain from taking what is not given; (3) to abstain from sexual misconduct;

(4) to abstain from lying or misleading speech; (5) to abstain from intoxicants (or drugs) that distort the functioning of the mind.

Our best authority for understanding what is intended in these precepts is Buddhaghosa, who especially illuminates the first four. The brief discussion that follows is based largely on his commentary.

The rule against the taking of life has enjoyed much comment during the centuries, with some authorities holding that it means literally that *nothing* is to be deliberately killed by us and others (recognizing that without the destruction of life of some sort we could not even sustain ourselves), arguing that "life" here means anything that breathes, thus making it permissible to kill plants and vegetables. In any event, it is the *deliberate* destruction of the life that is primarily referred to here; if life is taken by accident, the actual killing may not be regarded as an offense against *sīla,* but the negligence which made the accident possible decidedly comes up for judgment.

Since deliberate effort is the karmically bad ingredient in the act of killing, the intensity of the will and the amount of energy expended in the effort are significant for measuring the seriousness of the offense, and it follows —logically enough but a little grotesquely to the modern mind—that one is sometimes warned that the killing of large animals is more heinous than the killing of small ones. If a human being is the victim, the seriousness of the crime is affected by the degree of virtue that had been attained in the stricken life. But the most powerful factor in establishing the depth of guilt in the act of killing is simply the intensity of the desire to kill.

Buddhaghosa indicates that there are six ways in which the offense of killing may be perpetrated: with one's own

hand, by employing or instigating someone else, by missiles, by poisoning, by sorcery, or by the use of malevolent
psychic power.

"Taking what is not given" means appropriating something that one believes is the property of someone else.
This misappropriation may be accomplished in a variety of
ways, including simple theft, gambling, cheating, or strat-
agems designed to take advantage of another person. The
seriousness of the fault here depends partly on the worth
of the stolen or misappropriated property and partly on
the merit of its true owner, the man whom one has robbed.

Perhaps the most complex of these rules is that concerning sexual misconduct, for this phrase covers a number of
possible behaviors. Homosexuality is forbidden here, and
so is sexual relationship with women who fit certain
categories. Among the latter are women who have not
yet left their parental home, prostitutes, concubines, slaves,
prisoners of war, and "temporary wives." Nuns are taboo,
as is any woman who is under a vow of chastity, and one
may not enjoy intercourse with one's own wife in an un-
suitable locale, such as a public place or a shrine, or during
such inappropriate times as when she is nursing or during
pregnancy. Adultery is precluded, as is any form of sexual
aberration such as the use of a "forbidden passage."

The law against misleading speech is simple and
straightforward in intention: one must not deceive others
by one's words, gestures, inflection, or by any other means.
And the last of these precepts is, in some respects, similar
in aim to the fourth: the use of any agents which distort
the contents or functions of our mind is, in effect, to deceive ourselves just as a lie will deceive our friends. Truth-
fulness in one's representation of what one believes to be
the facts and honest, unafraid confrontation of reality in

one's own perceptions are sought in these last precepts.

Here, then, is the beginning of *sīla*. Faithful performance of the precepts will bring a man a long way on the
road to understanding, but it will not carry him completely
to that goal. At some time in his career it will, in the opinion of most Theravāda authorities, be necessary that a Buddhist become a monk, for only in that condition can one
find the time and the singleness of purpose to perfect the
more rigorous disciplines without which we cannot finally
be free from the fetters which hold us earthbound. What,
then, characterizes the *sīla* for a monk?

In accepting ordination a monk will make the usual
statement of faith in the Buddha, *dharma,* and *sangha,* and
will then formally accept the restraint of ten precepts—
the five we have already examined and five more with
which the layman is not troubled. These are, rather obviously, merely designed to discourage luxury and laxity
and tend to be rather less morally significant, from most
points of view, than the five precepts shared with laymen.
They are: (1) to abstain from eating after noon; (2) to
abstain from watching dancing, singing, and entertain-
ments in general; (3) to abstain from self-adornment with
flowers, spices, perfumes, etc.; (4) to abstain from using
a high bed; (5) to abstain from accepting or possessing
gold and silver.

More important than these additional precepts, however, is the fact that the monk now finds himself under
the authority of a very large body of additional rules expressly designed to govern the conduct of the *bhikkhu
sangha* of monks. These laws, referred to as the *Pātimokkha*
rules, number well over two hundred and are to be found
in the *Vinaya Piṭaka.* To discuss these injunctions would
take us far afield of our present project, but a reasonable

sample selection is to be found in Edward Conze's *Buddhist Scriptures*, Part Two, Chapter One.

The object of the entire body of *sīla* is to attack the most blatant of mankind's evil propensities—those which are manifested in overt action. We cannot progress far without the purification which the *sīla* can produce in our behavior, but the *sīla* alone is not enough to bring us to *Nirvāna*. There are more subtle defilements within our living, and there are qualities to perfect that need a different sort of discipline, so in addition to *sīla* the Theravāda offers us *samādhi:* the mental discipline of concentration.

Samādhi

Samādhi refers to the traditional sixth, seventh, and eighth elements of the Eightfold Path, Right Effort, Right Attentiveness, and Right Concentration. Its chief objectives are to overcome defilements within us that are less overt than observable behavior because they operate at the level of thought and feeling, and to attain tranquillity and insight.

As our competence in meditation develops, we find ourselves increasingly able to recognize and control our own motives, restraining those which would issue in undesirable behavior and thus attacking the problem of karmically disadvantageous action at its root. Further, there is a diminishment of certain disastrous personal qualities—laziness, restlessness, passion, doubt, and ill-will—and the progressive mastery by us of our mental operations. It is claimed that at last we may even acquire powers through advanced meditation which elude the ordinary levels of experience: clairvoyance, levitation, remembrance of past lives, the capacity to read the thoughts of others, and so on. But however gratifying the attainments along the way,

we must never lose sight of the great objectives of
our meditating, *samatha* ("tranquillity") and *vipassanā*
("intuitive vision" or "insight"). The latter is the ultimate
goal (opening the door as it does to that culmination of
the entire Buddhist venture, *Nirvāna*), and there are
many who argue today that the long and arduous path
to the former can be conveniently truncated, since
vipassanā is the comprehensive goal and *samatha* (considered separately) merely a stage in its attainment. Tradition, however, has usually placed the two together, and
we shall outline first the means and methods of achieving
the tranquil mind, and then discuss the final leap to
vipassanā.

The great tradition of Buddhist meditation offers us
forty subjects for contemplation, and it may be as well for
us to list these before outlining their function.[7]

Ten Devices
1. Earth Device: a circle made of clay
2. Water Device: a bowl of clear water
3. Fire Device: a flame
4. Air Device: something, such as the top of a tree,
   that can be seen to move in the breeze
5. Blue Device: some blue object such as a piece of
   cloth
6. Yellow Device: something yellow
7. Red Device: something red
8. White Device: something white
9. Light Device: a beam of light shining through a
   hole
10. Space Device: a limited space viewed through some
    aperture

Ten Impurities
1. A swollen corpse
2. A discolored, blue-green corpse
3. A corpse full of pus
4. A fissured corpse
5. A corpse torn by animals
6. A dismembered corpse
7. A scattered corpse
8. A blood-spattered corpse
9. A worm-infested corpse
10. A skeleton

Ten Recollections
Recollection of:
1. the Buddha's virtues
2. the merits of the *dharma*
3. the *bhikkhu sangha*
4. the merits of observing the precepts
5. the merits of liberality
6. the equality of gods and men in respect of the virtues
7. the inevitability of death
8. the body
9. breath
10. the attributes of mental tranquillity

The Four Sublime States
1. Universal benevolence
2. Compassion
3. The happiness of others
4. Equanimity

The Four Immaterial States
1. Infinite space

2. Infinite Consciousness
3. Nothingness
4. Neither perception nor non-perception

The two remaining subjects for meditation are:
1. The notion of the loathsomeness of food
2. The analysis of the four primary elements

Armed now with a list of recommended subjects for meditational exercises, we may proceed to a sketch of the pathway of meditation itself. In our progress toward tranquillity we must pass through three clear stages, namely, those of Preliminary, Access, and Attainment Concentration, or Meditation. Each deserves a note of explanation.

Preliminary Concentration. In the mastery of this first stage one must learn to sit properly (so that the body is controlled and unable to distract the mind) and to become largely insensitive to extraneous sensual stimuli. Any of the forty meditation subjects may become the focus upon which one bends one's attention as narrowly as possible, but some of them are more useful for specific kinds of personality than others. For instance, if the meditator is an impetuous, volatile sort of person, it is suggested that the four sublime states or the four color devices are most useful; for the unusually alert and quick-witted, mindfulness about the inevitability of death, the loathsomeness of food, or the constituents of mental tranquillity are recommended; and for the sensual among us there is meditation on the ten impurities and recollection of the body (and its vulnerability).

When the master under whose direction we are meditating has satisfied himself that the preliminary stage has been fully attained, we can proceed to Access Meditation.

Access Concentration. The achievement that signals success here is the entire elimination from our consciousness, during meditation, of almost all external stimuli, and the meditational subjects which are found to be most useful are the first eight "recollections," the notion of food's loathsomeness, and the analysis of the primary elements. A very high degree of competence in concentrating the mind upon a single subject without distraction having now been attained, we are ready to graduate to the third stage of competence.

Attainment Concentration. Any or all of the subjects not so far employed may be used in this stage, the perfection of which may take the beginner many lifetimes. There are, according to variant traditions, eight or nine substages within the sphere of Attainment Concentration, the first four (or five) of which belong to the realm of Form, and the last four to the Formless realm. For the various levels associated with Form one may use as meditational subjects the ten devices and the "recollection of breath" exercise, although other subjects are also useful. For the Formless attainments one must employ meditation on the four immaterial states.

All the substages in this category are often referred to as "absorptions" and are actually trance conditions which the adept learns, with much practice, to enter at will and to sustain for long periods (although none of them can ever be held permanently). The mastery of these absorptions, *dhyānas* (*jhānas*), produces the desired tranquillity but never the ultimate end of Buddhist aspiration—*Nirvāna* itself. As a result, and because the road to absorption is so long and arduous, there has arisen in recent years a tendency to bypass Attainment Concentration and move directly from Access Concentration to the kind of meditation that we have called *vipassanā*, or insight, the latter being, after all, the real goal of the entire process. What, then, is *vipassanā* meditation?

Vipassanā. This is the type of meditation which many Buddhists regard as distinctive to their tradition, since most or all of the elements in the pursuit of *samatha* are common to other systems, including some which are even older than Buddhism. Further, it is only *vipassanā* meditation that finally destroys craving and lifts us beyond mystical states which are merely "mind-produced" into the clear light of Absolute Truth. Here arises in us the *Nirvāna* experience.

Vipassanā is the full, intuitive insight into the impermanence (*anicca*), suffering (*dukkha*), and egolessness (Skt.: *anātman;* Pali: *anattā*) of everything, and it is therefore to be expected that the meditation which produces this effect centers upon impermanence, suffering, and egolessness. The interesting, and probably unexpected, fact that leads many Buddhist laymen to attempt *vipassanā* today without passing through all the *dhyānas* is that this ultimate accomplishment actually requires less meditational skill than the Attainment Concentration with its various stages.

The nature of *vipassanā* meditation has been excellently described in the following words:

> The meditator who seeks to practice the meditation which leads to insight, if he has already developed any of the levels of absorption, enters any stage of absorption and from it analyzes the factors and qualities of that stage and tries to understand their impermanence, suffering, and non-substantiality. If he has not attained any level of absorption, he will analyze his own life. Either way, he will see by analyzing his own self that the so-called being of self

is nothing but a process or flux of mental and material states which are interdependent. . . . At last he realizes the voidness or emptiness of the life of all living beings, either human or divine. The whole universe appears to him as a mere flux, as mere vibrations which are void of any entity. With the attainment of this realization, craving for such an existence wanes, vanishes, and ceases to be.[8]

When this insight and its consequent demolition of craving is complete, the meditator has reached the end of his road; he is an *Arhat*, an enlightened being who has completed the Theravāda pilgrimage. This means that the fulfillment of *vipassanā* is simultaneously the bursting forth in perfection of the final element in the so-called Threefold Training—*prajñā*, or wisdom.

Prajñā

Prajñā as a discipline may be thought of as synonymous with the "Right Understanding" and "Right Thought ("Mindedness")" of the Eightfold Path, and this means that it is not merely something that appears at the end of our journeying, but something that is consciously sought throughout.

At the stage that we have called Access Meditation, or Concentration, there *begins* to dawn an apprehension of the truth of the impermanence, egolessness, and consequent misery of life, and this becomes stronger as meditation continues and is gradually perfected. At last the Four Noble Truths become not didactic sentences that we understand as reasonable propositions but supra-verbal and intuitively embraced illuminations. When this is the case we are standing in the Truth; wisdom has been born in us and the pursuit of Right Understanding and Right

Thought has come to its end in the same moment when craving disappears. *Vipassanā*, the meditation toward insight, and *prajñā* reach their culminations at the same time and in those culminations become one.

Here, in too small a compass, we have examined the Way of Theravāda striving. It now remains for us only to glance for a moment at the Wayfarers—those who stand as the ideal exemplars of the process to enlightenment.

The Buddha

Foremost among those who have successfully trodden the Way is, of course, the Buddha himself—or, rather, the Buddhas themselves, for tradition lists others beside Gautama. In Theravāda teaching there are commonly held to have been three Buddhas in the present world age apart from Gautama, their names being Kassapa, Konagamana, and Kakusandha, and there is the promise of one more to come (Skt.: Maitreya; Pali: Metteya) who will initiate a revival of the true faith. When one begins to reckon with world ages other than ours, the number of accomplished Buddhas grows and becomes infinite.

To complicate Theravāda Buddhology we learn in many places in the Pali scriptures that there are several types of Buddha. Gautama was of the type known as *Pannadhika* ("Wisdom") Buddhas, but we read also of *Viriyadhika* ("Will Power") Buddhas, *Suddhadhika* ("Devotional") Buddhas, and *Pacceka* (Skt.: *Pratyeka*) ("Private" or "Silent") Buddhas. These are largely classified according to that supreme quality in them which is exemplified by their attainment. For instance a *Viriyadhika* Buddha achieves his glorious state by the exertion of untiring force of will for an incalculable period (eight world-cycle eras) and a *Pacceka* Buddha is successful privately—that is, without the benefit of having ever heard the word of a Buddha and without sharing his insight with anyone else. It may be noted that the *Pacceka* Buddha raises a problem for us, since Buddhist doctrine emphasizes that no sentient being can achieve a realization of the Truth and *Nirvāna* without hearing the teaching of a Buddha, yet there are examples, evidently, of exceptions to the rule. Of course, a more serious problem emerges as soon as we ask how the very first Buddha achieved understanding if a Buddha's teaching is necessary. There are inconsistencies here, and although it would be simplest to abandon the necessity of Buddha's teaching, Theravādins have not been willing to do that since their tradition is clear on the subject. They have preferred to dismiss our questions as unprofitable.

This plethora of Buddhas should not obscure the fact that, for Theravādins, it is the Buddha Gautama with whom we, in this time, have chiefly to deal, and Theravāda Buddhology is, naturally, most concerned with him. What sort of being was he? In what ways is he different from us? How should the faithful regard him and relate to him?

The first datum to be grasped is that the Buddha was a man; he was a man like us—yet like no one of us! He was the ideal man, the one who, through intense spiritual discipline, perfected in many life-spans, had attained enlightenment and even omniscience together with a considerable array of super-normal powers. However exalted in his perfections, he stands as the apex of a striving, after which we should model our own lives, for there is nothing in him that is not potential for each of us. He is not a god and is not to be worshiped; he is not present in some heaven as a personal being to whom the devout may pray for assistance. The Buddha stands as an example of human attainment; as the great Wayfarer who has drawn the map that we less accomplished travelers may follow.

The second datum that a student of Buddhism quickly discovers is that, at a very early period, the Buddha began to receive a veneration difficult to distinguish from that appropriate for deity. C. H. S. Ward observes:

> Buddhism, which began as an agnostic philosophy, was changing into a popular religion. When Gautama Buddha died, his relics were divided into seven parts, and seven *stupas,* sacred relic mounds, were erected over them. Pilgrimages to the *stupas* became common, and devout Buddhists bowed in adoring reverence before the relics.[9]

As early as the third century B.C., some *stupas* were becoming rather elaborate works of art, and by the first century A.D., the Buddha was being represented in sculpture that many people approached with great piety.

Even more remarkable, and more accessible to us, is the development of Buddhology within the Pali scriptures themselves. Perhaps in part as a defensive reaction to the emerging personalistic worship of Śiva and Vishnu in Hinduism, some of the scriptures present a Buddha who is marked from birth for ultimate attainment and stands, in some respects, as far above the rest of us as Mount Meru stands above the plain. I cannot forbear to quote at length the slightly astringent prose of A. B. Keith who sums up this development:

> In the *Mahapadana Suttana* of the *Dīgha Nikāya* we have the fullest and most categorical declaration of the transcendental character of the Buddha. He is no mere mortal reformer, but a sage whose divine insight enables him to pierce back to the ninety-first aeon ago when the Buddha Vipassin came to earth to be followed in the thirty-first

aeon by Sikhin and Yessabhu, and in this aeon by Kakusandha, Konagamana, and Kassapa, and finally by Gotama
himself. Theirs is no mortal birth; they descend in full
consciousness amid surpassing radiance throughout the
universe into their mother's womb. . . . At birth gods receive them, streams of water fall to bathe them, they stride
seven paces proclaiming their pre-eminence, the worlds
are illuminated; their mothers bear them standing and
without defilement, but die on the seventh day. The infants
bear already the marvellous marks, thirty-two in number,
which mark them out as Great Males, destined either to
become Emperors of the World or Buddhas, the flat feet,
the dustless skin, the long tongue, the mole between the
eyebrows, and the turban-like protruberance on the head.
. . . No two Buddhas can coexist, and it is the privilege
of the Buddha to extend his life to the full length of an
aeon; shame on Ananda who in heedlessness failed to
accept the hint repeatedly pressed on him by Gotama, and
to beg his master to exercise this power, instead of passing
away at the age of eighty, like a mere man.[10]

Here is a remarkable picture indeed, and it has been
argued that it cannot be entirely due to the fervor of pious
imagination but must have had at least its seeds in
Gautama's own understanding of himself. He is, for instance, reported to have said:

The All-subduing, the all-knowing am I, in everything that
I am, without a spot. I have given up everything; I am
without desire, a delivered one. By my own power I
possess knowledge; whom shall I call my master? I have
no teacher; no one is to be compared with me. In the world,
including the heavens, there is no one like me. I am the
Holy One in the world. I am the Supreme Master. I alone
am the perfect Buddha.[11]

One cannot, of course, guarantee that the Buddha actually said this of himself, but if he did not, someone at a fairly early date found it not inappropriate to put these words in his mouth posthumously.

Quite early, too, come stories of his astonishing powers:

> At that time the river Ganges was brimful and overflowing; and wishing to cross to the opposite bank, some began to seek for boats, some for rafts of wood, whilst some made rafts or basket-work. Then the Exalted One, as instantaneously as a strong man would stretch forth his arm, or draw it back when he had stretched it forth, vanished from this side of the river and stood on the further bank.[12]

Already in the Pali scriptures, then, we seem to see the development of qualities in the Buddha that make it difficult for us to think of him merely as a self-fulfilled human being. As we shall see, Mahāyāna Buddhology carried this process even farther. But, for Theravāda at least, it remains true that in principle the Buddha's attainments are potential for any sentient being who will follow the Way to its very end. And what an end that is! When we have reached it we shall find ourselves not merely far above all mortal men, but above the gods, too, for they are mortal like the rest of us and, unlike the Buddha, distinctly limited in understanding, as the following charming story indicates.

A monk was one day greatly puzzled by a metaphysical problem to which he could find no solution, so he decided to consult the great god Brahma. He found Brahma in the company of a retinue of lesser deities and approached him with due respect, asking: "Where do the elements cease and leave no trace behind?" Brahma replied, "I am the Great Brahma, the Supreme, the Mighty, the All-

Seeing, the Ruler, the Lord of All, appointing each to his place, the Father of all that are and that are to be." "Yes," said the monk, "but I did not ask you what you were, I asked where the four elements cease and leave no trace." Then Brahma took the monk by the arm and led him aside. When they were in private the divinity said: "These gods think I know everything, and that is why I did not answer you in front of them. The truth is, I *cannot* answer your question. You had better go and ask the Buddha." [13]

The attainment of Buddhahood is a splendid and lofty end for human effort. So exalted is it, indeed, that it has virtually been eliminated as a realistic goal for Theravādins and replaced by a humbler one: the achievement of a lesser degree of enlightenment which is still adequate for the enjoyment of *Nirvāna*. The name for the attainer of this state is *Arhat*.

The Arhat

The *Arhat* ("one who is worthy") is an exalted being. Stanislav Schayer says of him:

> The Buddhist saint, the Arhat, not to mention a Buddha, stands as high as heaven above the world; he does not despise the world, but he also does not love it; he pities it only, and again not in the Christian sense of fellow-feeling and of being inside the sinful world, but from without, as an onlooker who has himself escaped from the misery and looks down on striving humanity in the full consciousness of his own further immunity from suffering.[14]

Unlike a Buddha, an *Arhat* is not omniscient. Indeed, it is generally assumed that his understanding is less complete than that of a *Pacceka* Buddha but it is sufficient for the accomplishment of *Nirvāna* because it is free from all ignorance that entails passion or defilement. The *Arhat* does not comprehend the complexity of universal being as a Buddha does, and he does not know the distant past or future, but such knowledge is not essential to deliverance from birth and death.

Nor does the *Arhat* possess the distinguishing physical marks of a Buddha, or the latter's miraculous powers. But he is undeceived about suffering and its origin, and he knows that for him *saṃsāra* is overcome.

Since the description of the *Arhat* belongs properly to the category of "character development" and the analysis of the Buddhist Way belongs largely to ethics, we shall pursue them no farther so far as Theravāda is concerned; our purpose in extending this discussion beyond the boundaries of philosophy has been the building of a framework for Buddhist philosophy, and this having been achieved, we must leave the completion of the present topics for another study. First, however, we should again turn to Mahāyāna to see in what ways its distinctive metaphysics reshaped the concepts of the Way and the Wayfarer.

MAHĀYĀNA

Like Theravāda, Mahāyāna Buddhism attacks the twin problems of desire and ignorance but tends to emphasize the latter as the principal target. It is argued that if the control of desire or appetite were primary, Gautama would doubtless have followed other Indian teachers in recommending stringent asceticism whereas, in fact, he renounced extremes of self-denial as much as indulgence. Desire arises because we see the world through the prism of illusion and our effort must be to correct this. This does not mean that the problem of craving is ignored; on the contrary, control of desire is still important, but it is very clearly a means to an end beyond itself.

Sīla, for Mahāyāna, aims at achieving a state of purity in us that will permit us to break through all illusion and see the Truth. It is not really the case that there is something for us to learn but, in an almost Platonic fashion, our task is to remove the obstructions of ignorance and error, for when this has been done the Truth appears or, rather, is disclosed. It is important to emphasize this functional value of sīla, for an important consequence of it is that if the ultimate goal (attainment of enlightenment) should ever be facilitated by means of the suspension of sīla, that suspension would be justified. Mahāyāna produces an attitude toward ethics, then, interestingly similar in at least one respect to Søren Kierkegaard's, for the latter's famous doctrine of the "teleological suspension of the ethical" echoes in Christian terms the relative position of ethics in Mahāyāna.

Six Cardinal Virtues

We noted earlier that Theravāda discusses a set of five cardinal virtues. Mahāyāna, too, has its list of virtues and these are usually six in number: giving, morality, patience, vigor, concentration, and wisdom. It is to be noted that this list goes beyond the content of sīla itself, and wisdom, when perfect, is precisely that illumination whose fullness means the completion of all the others in the perfect attainment of illumination. It is not the case that one perfects these virtues in sequence but, rather, that all must be cultivated together. Very briefly, the content of each of these virtue concepts is as follows.

1. Giving (*dāna*): This is the perfect expression of detachment from transient things, for it refers to the giving of articles and even of one's own body and life to meet the needs of others. Included in the concept is the highly virtuous act of giving (that is, teaching) the *dharma* itself. Even the merit, conceived of almost as a power, earned by these other acts of generosity should be given: it should be dedicated to the attainment of enlightenment not only for oneself but for all sentient beings.

2. Morality (*sīla*): In essence this refers to the faithful following of the ten great precepts against killing, stealing, fornicating, lying, slandering, speaking harshly, speaking flippantly, coveting, entertaining aggressive thought, and erroneous views.

3. Patience (*ksānti*): One should always suffer adversity and cruelty patiently, and should submit to Buddhism's most unwelcome ideas willingly.

4. Vigor (*vīrya*): It is the appropriate employment of energy that is virtuous. Not merely being busy, but energetically combating one's own faults and the evils that surround one; improving the store of merit in the world and, by serious study of the *dharma*, improving one's own approach to understanding are the kind of activities upon which vigor is virtuously expended.

5. Concentration or Meditation (*dhyāna*): One must learn to master the disciplines and trances of concentration until they are perfected, yet not allow oneself to be seduced into accepting the withdrawal from the common human problem they may make possible. The skills perfected here are not for oneself alone but should facilitate one's contributing to the perfection of all beings.

6. Wisdom (*prajñā*): In its perfection this is the state

in which one has attained the Truth so fully that the Truth, the knower, and the knowing are no longer separate entities but indivisible. None of the other virtues can be perfected until this last reaches its fruition. This provokes a logical difficulty, as we shall see more fully when we consider the Mahāyāna *bodhisattva*, for the fullness of wisdom (in which all distinctions and otherness are overcome) and the fullness of giving (which presupposes otherness) seem difficult to reconcile. No doubt it was such a difficulty which led Theravāda thinkers to make compassion subservient to wisdom and a virtue to be finally surmounted.

Here, then, is the shape of Mahāyāna character-development theory. The absolutism of Mahāyāna reveals itself in the tendency, already suggested, for every virtue to be drawn into the perfection of one—wisdom—even at the cost of logical precision. This is a point deserving further explication, however, and we shall examine it now from a new perspective.

If one asks for a discussion of Mahāyāna ethics, in order to see how Buddhist absolutism affects these, we can do no better than to consider the teaching of the great thirteenth-century Japanese scholar Dōgen, probably the profoundest thinker produced by the Buddhism of that land and a man whom some consider worthy to rank with such great Mahāyāna figures as Nāgārjuna, Asanga, and Vasubandhu. In Dōgen's important but difficult book entitled *Shōbō-genzō* there is a chapter (*Shoakumakusa*) which specifically treats the subject of ethics and the following discussion attempts to follow his argument closely but not exhaustively. (I am indebted for the translation of the relevant material, together with whatever I have understood of it, to Professor Hiroshi Sakamoto of Otani University in Kyoto, who labored long and with great *karunā* to make Dōgen's point of view available to me.)

Dōgen speaks eloquently about the Buddha-Nature and this term is a favorite synonym with him for what we have usually called *Śūnyatā*. The Buddha-Nature is, to use Western terms, the Absolute Reality that persists behind the mists of our deluded egotism and of the ephemeral world of transient and particular realities. When all that is illusion is gone, this is what remains; when all that can die is dead, this is what survives; when all false meanings are dispelled, this is the Truth. How does he relate ethical theory to this basic metaphysical entity?

Dōgen begins the chapter from which we are drawing our present ideas by quoting a familiar passage that occurs in several places throughout Buddhist scriptures:

> The Buddha said,
> Do not commit evil;
> Do good devotedly;
> Purify your mind.

Having stated his text, so to speak, Dōgen next isolates the first part of it—"Do not commit evil"—and begins to expound its meaning at some length. He does the same, subsequently, for each section of the verse, but we shall have space only to consider his treatment of this first line. Since this, however, will produce the essence of his view of ethics we can be satisfied.

Every Buddha, it seems, has left us this injunction against evil. On the face of it, it seems both a trivial and an imprecise command and suggests the image of the faithful Buddhist as a sort of simpleminded Oriental

Puritan preoccupied with the negative function of avoiding whatever orthodoxy disapproves. Dōgen, however, sees this injunction in quite a different way. It is important not because it is a piece of good, if pedestrian, advice, but because it is pregnant with ontological illumination. To put the matter briefly, "Commit no evil" is the self-expression of the Buddha-mind, and the practice of it is that same mind itself in action. He says: "This 'Do not commit evil' is not something contrived by any mere man. It is the *Bodhi* [the supreme enlightenment] turned into words. . . . It is the [very] speaking of enlightenment." [15]

The significance of this is that the enlightenment spoken of here cannot be separated from Ultimate Reality itself. It is an important Mahāyāna understanding that the Absolute and the *knowing* of the Absolute are identical—the knowing and the being are one. Consequently to say that "Do not commit evil" is the speech of *Bodhi* means that it is the self-expression of the Absolute. Having established this, Dōgen goes on: "Being moved by the supreme enlightenment one learns to aspire to commit no evil, to put this injunction into practice, and as one does so the practise-power emerges which covers all the earth, all worlds, all time, and all existences without remainder."

This is rather unclear, to be sure, but it seems to mean that the "practise-power" which is manifested as the Buddhist applies himself to avoiding evil is not simply the inherent power of the individual, but the power of the Absolute. In short, "Do not commit evil" is both the *verbal* self-expression of the Absolute and its *active* self-expression as well. The command to perform and the power to perform are essentially identical, and this unity of command and performance is rooted in the unborn Buddha-Nature. Dōgen's way of putting it is picturesque:

A pine-tree in spring is neither non-existent nor existent,
but it is [absolutely] the "do not commit"; a chrysanthemum in autumn is neither existent nor non-existent, but it
is [absolutely] "do not commit"; Buddhas are neither
existent nor non-existent, but they are the "do not commit";
a pillar, a lantern, a brush, a stick are none of them
existent nor non-existent, but [absolutely] "do not commit."

What is meant here, of course, is that a pine tree, for example, should be seen not as a natural object only, but
more importantly as the "do not commit," that is, as another manifestation of that same Ultimate which is the
reality of both the command not to commit evil and the
power to obey it. In other words, particularity, as we find
it in the command, and in the power to act, and in the
action itself, in a pine tree, a chrysanthemum, and so on
indefinitely is, even while it is genuine particularity, nevertheless the Absolute. Particularity has existed from beginningless time, yet it is also true that the unborn Buddha-
Nature encompasses all particularities in such a way that
while not destroying them, it is itself not divided by them.

All this raises the trite sentence "Do not commit evil"
to a new and surprising level of complexity and importance. It is not merely a rule of behavior, it is the way in
which that which eternally *is* expresses its character, and
therefore I must consider myself in some degree of alienation from Truth and Reality whenever it is a self-conscious
struggle on my part to obey. "Do not commit evil" must
become my subjectivity. It must not remain an externally
imposed rule. And when it is truly my subjectivity and my
true self, then that self is no longer the separate, finite ego
of which I once boasted, but is no other than the Unborn,
the Absolute, the Eternal Truth.

But here we find the problem of evil arising for us again.

In a system of philosophy that identifies the particulars of existence with an indivisible Reality, is not evil also that Reality? If it is not, then it clearly cannot have reality at all.

In a rather difficult passage Dōgen says: "Examining the problem of the evil referred to, three kinds of disposition are to be distinguished: the good, the evil and the neutral. The evil is (indeed) one of them. Nevertheless, the evil disposition is, as much as the good and the neutral, in its essence birthless. They are all birthless, immaculate and finally real."

Hiroshi Sakamoto interprets this as meaning that the Unborn is the reality of all that is. Consequently when a mind turns to evil, even that by which and with which it does evil (its energies and so on) must be the Unborn. Not only the good, but also the evil disposition is birthless and immaculate. Its quality as "evil" is not finally, decisively, or ontologically alien to the Absolute but is merely a form in which that reality finds expression in the realm of relativity.

In Dōgen's thought we find the affirmation of the inviolability of Reality in its Absoluteness: it is untouched by evil, untarnished by the thousand shapes of horror that men know. Yet in the sphere of multiplicity, the world in which particulars relate to each other and relativize each other and all actions, evil genuinely exists. And since what matters is that enlightenment should break out throughout the relative and evil-haunted level of empirical existence rather than that evil should be recompensed and punished, it follows that whenever we must operate at this empirical level, our obligation is not merely to do good in a selective or amorphous fashion, but especially to do that good which will provoke the awakening of any of our fellows anywhere. The behavior of the individual must, therefore, be dictated by the impulse to do good rather than evil, but that good especially which leads to the universalizing of truth-seeing; for when the Truth is seen by all, there will be no more good to do since there will be no more evil: the Truth is beyond good and evil, and our goal must be that condition in which the Truth alone remains.

We see in Dōgen, then, a skillful attempt to relate Mahāyāna subjectivism and ontology to some primary questions of ethics: Whence comes value and what is the relation of being and doing? Dōgen finds the Absolute to be his authentic Self, and this means that both the command to do no evil and the power to obey it are our Self. When we have overcome the illusion of isolated individuality we know that the age-old problem of relating being and doing, ethics and moral action, or command and power to obey is overcome. The enlightened man acts spontaneously and properly, for his acting is his being and both are the Truth. Moreover, the very struggle to live according to *sīla* may now be seen as itself a deliberate movement toward the appropriation of the truth about Reality, for the degree to which my adherence in action to recognized Buddhist standards of behavior is spontaneous is the degree to which I have moved from error to understanding.

The introduction of a notion of Absolute Reality may be seen, then, greatly to influence Mahāyāna ethical theory. Even more remarkable is its modification of soteriology.

The Buddha has taught that self-help is the only road to enlightenment, and Theravāda has understood this individualistically. But if there is no true self except the Void, and if this is everyone's authentic Selfhood, what does self-help mean? Suddenly it appears that *karma* and ignorance can no longer be considered individual calamities, for individuality is too frail an illusion to bear their weight. *Karma* must be a transpersonal phenomenon, and ignorance a cloud that cannot be divided into segments of "yours" and "mine." Similarly, then, merit of every kind must belong to *all* rather than to any one "being." Enlightenment must, in some important sense, be universal rather than particular.

Already in Theravāda we find the appearance of a doctrine of merit transference implying that the fruits of worthy action may be transferred to the service of another being. But it is in Mahāyāna that this concept is developed extensively, for it was one way to approach the implications for spiritual progress of the concept of the ubiquitous Buddha-Nature, and the consequently universal character of true enlightenment.

At its simplest level the doctrine of *parivarta*, or *parināmana* ("turning over" or "transference"), means that merit established anywhere and by anyone may be devoted to the benefit of another, or to the universalizing of enlightenment. Of course, this transference occurs in the illusion-ridden phenomenal realm of perception, and it *can* occur there precisely because in final truth the individualistic distinctions of that realm are illusory. If *Śūnyatā* is the non-dual Reality, it is clear that merit applies to *it* and therefore properly to every manifestation of it. This commonality of merit, exemplified by the notion of transference, is an inevitable outcome of Absolutism in the Buddhist frame of reference.

At first the general idea of merit transferability meant that one person could offer his own merit to others, but a philosophical or soteriological "breakthrough" occurred when Buddhists of the "Pure Land" traditions realized that the doctrine might also imply the transference to an individual of the limitless merit of a Buddha. With this perception a way of deliverance appeared even for those who despaired of ever dispelling the fog of discriminating illusion, and Buddhism acquired a gospel that in some respects is curiously similar to its Christian counterpart. Here, henceforth, was to be found a notion of "salvation by grace through faith." The development of this idea was pushed to its logical limit in the teaching of the Jōdo Shin Shū ("True Pure Land") sect and it may be profitable to follow their reasoning for a moment, since theirs is the numerically strongest form of Mahāyāna in the world today.

As in Buddhism generally, Jōdo Shin teaches that man's basic problem is a terrible ignorance. He does not know that his true nature consists in identity with the Absolute, and consequently he falsely imputes to himself a self-existent particular ego and develops a dualistic frame of mind in which the polarity of subject and object becomes the norm of thought and experience. How, then, do we escape into truth and peace?

Traditionally the Buddhist answer to our dilemma has indicated that the escape route was the Threefold Discipline (morality, meditation, wisdom) or some variant of this. Shin, however, arose largely because of a feeling of the insurmountable difficulties of the hard road preached by these conventional disciplines, a difficulty intensified by the steady (and predicted) degeneration of mankind since the days of Śākyamuni. Shinran, the founder of the Jōdo Shin sect in Japan, was himself acutely aware of his own inability to achieve the desirable moral perfection. He wrote:

This self who is unable to distinguish right from wrong, good from evil, who has no claim even for little deeds of love and compassion, and yet who is willing just for name and gain to pose as teacher [how shameful]! [16]

It was, then, with a sense of profound release that Shinran heard from the great Pure Land teacher Hōnen of the possibility of another way, the road of faith. To grasp the Shin Shū development of the merit-transference idea, we will find it useful to ask a series of questions: If Pure Land Buddhism is a Buddhism of faith, who is the object of that faith? What is the mechanism by which the faith becomes effective? What is the relationship of the faith to meritorious work and to *karma*? How is faith experienced?

The Object of Faith

"Amida" is the Japanese name for the Buddha known throughout the Mahāyāna world by the names Amitābha and Amitāyus. At one level he may be thought of as a man who, after countless lives of striving, reached perfection long before Gautama. As a *bodhisattva* ("saint") he had vowed to establish, through his accumulated merits, a "pure land" to which all who called upon him in faith might subsequently be reborn and in which all obstacles to their attainment of enlightenment and deliverance would be removed.

At another level, however, he (like every other human Buddha) is a manifestation of the Absolute itself. As Shinran says: "From the treasure-sea of the Absolute Oneness came the one incarnating himself as a *bodhisattva* called Dharmakara, and this personage, by having started the Vow which nothing can obstruct, and finally fulfilling it became the Buddha Amida." [17]

Amida, then, is the briefly incarnate but customarily both transcendent and immanent expression of the Ultimate Reality, that unborn and undying Suchness in which we all live and move and have our being, and which, indeed, in a profound sense, we all are. To have faith in him means that we rely on him as the means as well as the end of our salvation.

The Mechanism of Faith

We have already glanced at the notion of merit transference. This is the basis on which the gracious power of Amida is conceived as being effective in the lives of contemporary individuals. In the second part of the *Sukhāvātīvyūha Sūtra*, Śākyamuni tells Ānanda that if a man heard the name of Amida and even once turned to him in thought, he would be assured of rebirth in the Pure Land. Now, some Mahāyānists had interpreted this "turning toward" Amida as the act of dedicating one's store of personal merit to the hope of rebirth in Amida's land. Shinran, however, dramatically turned the merit transference idea upside down and argued that when a man turns to Amida, it is the Buddha who directs *His* unfathomable and inexhaustible merit toward the achievement of that man's hope. Thus the act of faith is, in effect, the acceptance of a gift of grace whereby eventual enlightenment is assured.

Faith, Works, and Karma

As in Christianity, there arose in Pure Land Buddhism a controversy over the necessity of pious "works" to supplement the faith of the believer. Is one assured of Amida's grace by mere faith, or must one perform certain acts as well? The basic assumption of the Shin version of Pure Land Buddhism is that faith *alone* obtains for us the benefit of Amida's power. Indeed, Shinran is as emphatic as the Christian Luther that to introduce any other element is a relapse from the purity of faith and an act of bad faith. In one of his hymns Shinran sings:

> Hearing the Name of the Buddha Amida,
> If one praises it with a deep joy,
> He will instantly obtain the supreme benefit,
> And be filled with treasures of merit.

When we realize that "hearing" here has a rather technical sense, and involves understanding the implications of Amida's will for men, believing in it, and trustfully yielding to it, we see how radical in terms of other forms of Buddhism Shinran's appears to be. Kenshō Yokogawa observes that adherents of other forms of Buddhism "first hear the teaching of Buddhism, then think about it and lastly carry it into practice, in order to obtain Buddha-wisdom, extirpating all their evil passions with their own efforts and labours." By contrast, he points out, "in Shin hearing only is necessary, for thinking and practice are vicariously done on the part of Amida." [18]

To indicate clearly the difference of its concept from that of other modes of Buddhism, Shin uses the terms *tariki* ("other-power") and *jiriki* ("self-power"). Wherever one relies wholly or in part on anything one can do to merit salvation, one is exhibiting *jiriki*—depending upon oneself. But the inherent difficulty of casting down the illusion of self by the effort of self must be obvious; such a policy is much more likely to result in self-delusion than anything else. So Shin stands firmly on the principle of *tariki*. The power to obtain rebirth in Amida's land and

consequent enlightenment is Amida's own power and
nothing else is of the slightest use. D. T. Suzuki points
out that Shinran was fond of saying that what is necessary
is that one cast oneself upon Amida's Vow (to deliver all
who called upon him) and then be perfectly "natural."
To be natural (*jinen*) in this context "means to be free
from self-willed intention, to be altogether trusting in the
Original Vow, to be absolutely passive in the hands of
Amida." [19] This passivity does not, however, imply moral
indifference or antinomianism, for although it is true that
no number of good works can save us, we must nevertheless not flaunt evil. In the *Tannishō* an anecdote concerning Shinran is recounted. The great man heard once of a
Buddhist who apparently thought that since Amida's grace
overcame all evil and Amida's Vow was expressly for evil-
doers, there was advantage in actually doing evil since
this brought one directly under the influence of the Vow.
Shinran promptly disabused the fellow by writing,
"Though a remedy may be at hand one must not take
poison." [20]

Good works are, then, of value, but not as a means to
salvation. They may express our gratitude for Amida's
Vow and our awakening to the needs of others, but they
do not buy Amida's grace.

Related to the question of pious work is the larger question of *karma:* In what way is action and its inevitable
karmic consequence modified by Shin faith? In one sense
it is not modified at all. We still live our mundane life in
the grip of *karma,* for there is no avoiding this. Yet by
the grace of Amida we are enabled to live simultaneously
this worldly life of *karma* and a life of spiritual freedom.
At the relative level of existence *karma* continues to con-

dition the pattern of our life, but we have discovered that Amida, who is Suchness itself, is no prisoner, and since we, in the absolute realm, are identified with him in the state of faith, we too transcend it. For as long as earthly life continues, then, we are content to let *karma* have its way, for it is Amida who, embracing us, filling us, becoming us, is the real *karma*-bearer, and Amida bears it willingly and, simultaneously, transcends it.

How Is Faith Experienced?

Faith in Shin is not mere belief. Nor is it simple obedience to a norm. As in most Christian thought, faith includes these but also entails an immediacy of encounter between the self and the religious object, an immediacy in which the very duality of self and object vanishes.

Further, the awakening of faith may be felt as a sort of impulsive leap which takes one beyond the process of intellection. Yet "leap" is hardly the correct word, for if it were, we would ourselves be responsible for it, whereas faith is Amida's gift. This does not mean that we may not have striven for faith, but when it occurs we know that all that has been done for our salvation was, in some important sense, done *for* us even as it was done *by* us.

But Shin faith is more than just a meeting of two egos. Rather it is an experience in which my relative and finite ego is discovered to be the secondary, dependent, conditioned, and essentially even illusory thing that it is, and I break through it to escape its cramping confinement in a union with that Absolute Self which is expressed in Amida.

The situation we are describing may be roughly expressed diagrammatically.

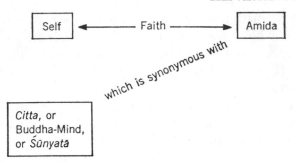

When the self awakens to faith in Amida, it awakens, too, to its own depth. It finds itself transformed. It is no longer the palpitating inconsequence it had always been, but finds that petty ego banished and replaced by the unfathomable *Citta*, or Buddha-Mind. It knows then that this Buddha-Mind is the Void and is Amida himself. Thus the truth of the adventure of faith is that the "other" in whom we found faith is ultimately not an "other" at all! This is the point at which Jōdo Shin thought reveals itself as not alien to Mahāyāna in general. The goal is precisely that sought by other Mahāyāna sects—realization of *Śūnyatā*—but the way to that goal is psychologically different. We have transcended the enormous difficulty of strenuous moral and intellectual effort by an act of commitment that brought us to the same goal.

Thus Mahāyāna offers us a variety of "ways" which are, nevertheless, all *The Way*. Zen's meditation, the devout employment of *śīla*, and the "simple" faith of Jōdo Shin are ways, more or less effective for different individuals, of treading the path to illumination. But it is clear that the Mahāyāna way offers significant deviation from that of Theravāda: Can the same be said of those exemplary Wayfarers—Buddhas and saints—as Mahāyāna conceives them?

MAHĀYĀNA BUDDHOLOGY ·

We have seen that already in the Pali scriptures the Buddha Gautama had acquired the stature of a wonder-worker who could hardly be regarded as simply an enlightened man. The Mahāyāna schools continued the development of Buddhology until an elaborate identification was effected between this venerated person and the concept of the Void itself. The Buddha begins, at last, to become supra-historical, and as his cosmic dimensions are made more clear his purely mundane ones diminish in importance, until the earthly Buddha comes to be regarded much as was the Christ in the Christian heresy known as Docetism. In fact, it is interesting to note that just as Christians tried to rationalize their supra-rational experience of God's presence in Christ and in the lives of believers by a doctrine of Trinity, Buddhists have sought to explicate *their* experience of the Buddha-Truth in a doctrine of *Trikāya*—meaning literally "three bodies" or, more adequately, three manifestations of the eternal and indivisible Truth.

As centuries passed, Buddhists pondered the meaning not only of the Master's words but of his being. Surely the two could hardly be separated, each in part deriving its authority from the other and both together constituting a unity of meaning. With the dawning of its absolutism the question of the significance of the Buddha's person became more insistent to Mahāyāna, but at the same time a marvelous light of understanding seemed to break. Of course the teaching of the Buddha and the being of the Buddha were one: "Enough, Vakkali, what is there to be seen in this putrid body of mine? Who sees Dharma, he sees me. Who sees me, he sees Dharma." [21] More than this, in that realm of understanding where no distinctions are seen, there could persist no divergence between the Buddha and the Absolute. Yet at the level of relative experience one could speak of the Buddha, of the Absolute, and even of that mystical apprehension of Buddha or Buddhas in which great saints rejoiced. Was it possible to reconcile the ultimate non-duality of Truth with these experiences? The attempt to reconcile them is the intriguing doctrine of *Trikāya*.

Briefly the *Trikāya* concept credits the Buddha-Truth with three forms, modes, or manifestations: (1) The *Dharmakāya*, or "Truth-body," the essence of all Buddhas, Buddhahood itself, the Absolute. (2) The *Sambhogakāya*, or "Enjoyment-body." This is the radiant form in which Buddhas appear to the enlightened and enraptured spiritual vision of saints. (3) *Nirmānakāya*, or "Transformation-body." Here is the earthly, material mode of the Truth's appearing—the "human" Buddha. It will repay us to consider each of these concepts briefly.

Dharmakāya

Dharmakāya is the Ultimate Reality, *Śūnyatā*, spoken about in Buddhological terms. Philosophers may be content to talk in cold abstractions, but most of us long for something to adore, something that seems a little less indifferent to us than an inclusive "Void." From one point of view we may say that the *Dharmakāya* represents the first step in a process whereby the impersonal Absolute is shown to be relevant for suffering humanity, for although it is true that it is merely another way of naming the nameless Ultimate, its usefulness consists in that there is already a suggestion of compassion, of reaching toward the isolated human unit in the use of this word. As we shall see, when *Dharmakāya* is recognized as itself needing to be supplemented by the *Sambhogakāya* and *Nirmānakāya* concepts we see that a kind of conceptual ladder has been built between the individual and the Ultimate, for that Buddha who spoke the kindly words of Truth below is none other, in essence, than the *Dharmakāya*.

When one thinks of the *Dharma*-body of the Buddha, in Mahāyāna, one thinks of an idea that performs for us some of the psychological functions of "God" in Western traditions, or "Brahman" for Hinduism. As with each of these, *Dharmakāya* is the ultimate ground of all that is, the one point of genuine aseity. Yet *Dharmakāya* is also unlike these rival concepts. It is unlike the Judeo-Christian God, for instance, in that it is not creative and not transcendental to a world of its intending. God is both immanent in the world and mysteriously transcendent of it; *Dharmakāya* is that of which the world is a manifestation. And *Dharmakāya* differs from Brahman in that it is less clearly impersonal: although it cannot be thought of as a person, it is the root of *karunā* and *prajñā* and Buddhists feel that it is a more dynamic concept than Brahman. Nor is it, at least for the Mādhyamikan strand of Mahāyāna, a pure *One*, for the Truth can be neither One nor Two, and this means that if Brahmanism is a neat philosophical monism, the *Dharmakāya* idea cannot be reconciled with it.

Dharmakāya, then, is the non-dual cosmic reality conceived as an object of religious consciousness. It is *Śūnyatā;* it is *Nirvāna;* it is *samsāra*. But as a *concept* it performs the function of offering to our minds an objectification

of Truth and Reality with enough warmth to draw us out
of our frail and frightened isolation.

It should be noted that in some schools of Mahāyāna the
name *Vairocana*-Buddha is often preferred to *Dhar-*
makāya, and sometimes the title *Ādibuddha* ("primal
Buddha") is used. In general, these refer to the same concept that we have been discussing, although there are some
minor differences in the ways in which different sectarian
traditions prefer to think about them. They have unique
technical meanings in Tibetan religion which, in any case,
is sufficiently different from other forms of Buddhism that
Buddhists often prefer to call it Lamaism.

Sambhogakāya

The *Sambhogakāya* is an idea rather more obscure than
Dharmakāya. Perhaps its meaning can best be approached
functionally, for it is doubtful whether the idea would have
arisen if it had not seemed desirable to account for certain
experiences claimed by or for exalted spirits. When the
saint, in mystical trance, seems to encounter the Buddha
and learns at first hand a new appreciation of old truths it
is the *Sambhoga*-body of Buddhahood he has met. There
are descriptions of the amazing forms in which this body
appears to be faithful: it is resplendent in light and glory
and the title given it, "Enjoyment-body," seems to indicate
the belief that this "body" is in part the symbol of the conviction that the attainment of enlightened Buddhahood
brings with it untroubled joy of a kind so different from
any which the mere mortal can experience that we have no
suitable words to describe it.

There are many stories of supernatural appearances of
the Buddha and in general we may apply the term

Sambhogakāya to them all as a convenient classificatory device. It represents something less than the *Dharmakāya* and something more than the earthly, physically limited Buddha. It is in the form of *Sambhogakāya* that the Buddha-Truth preaches most of the Mahāyāna *sūtras*, although the Shingon sect is unique in claiming its distinctive teachings to be the proclamation of the *Dharmakāya* directly.

In short, the function of the *Sambhogakāya* is first to symbolize the self-enjoyment of Buddhahood and second to be the locus of mystical instruction and enlightenment. As such it is another link between the unimaginable Ultimate and the limping consciousness of the earthbound man.

Nirmānakāya

Nirmānakāya was originally a Yogācārin word, the Mādhyamikans preferring *Rūpakāya,* or "form-body." Its essential reference is to the physical body of a Buddha, to the Buddha as a man.

The *Nirmānakāya*-Buddha is the Absolute as it manifests itself in an enlightened man for the benefit of other people. As such, the Absolute reveals itself as not entirely transcendent even of the corruption that prevails among us, for a *Nirmānakāya* must achieve enlightenment in our midst, moving from our ignorance to his perfect vision. As an ancient Chinese text important to Pure Land tradition puts it: "Manifesting himself in the world where five corruptions prevail, he follows the ways of those multifarious beings who are living there. Showing that he himself is defiled, he performs purification in the waters of the Golden River." [22] The five corruptions referred to here are the corruption of time (that is to say, the existence of degenerate ages in which such calamities as war, famine, and ignorance prevail), the corruption of thought and belief, of feeling (in evil passions), of the person (in weak character and inadequate bodies), and of life (which is brief because of degeneracy). The *Nirmānakāya* is, thus, the Buddha-Truth as it appears in a degenerate age to restore the vision of wholeness. Gautama is an example to us in our world of a *Nirmānakāya* in its fullness, but Japanese Buddhism makes an interesting distinction between this unalloyed version (which it calls *Ojin*) and a kind of partial *Nirmānakāya* (*keshin*), that is, an ordinary mortal who is distinguished by extraordinary saintliness. The founders of Mahāyāna sects tend to be regarded as *keshin*.

Conclusion

We see, then, in the *Trikāya* doctrine an attempt to give comfort to those who deplore the remoteness of an Absolute, and an attempt to rationalize the forms in which Buddha-Truth has been experienced. As T. R. V. Murti states: "Simultaneous with the revolution in Buddhism which changed it from the radical pluralism of the Hinayana to the absolutism of the Mahayana, there was felt the need for a mediating principle between the absolute and phenomenal beings. Buddha is that mediator."[23] And it is the *Trikāya* doctrine that tries to establish the validity and manner of the Buddha's mediation. Buddhas may be many in the numberless ages of existence, but they are all the appearance of the undivided Void. In the *Lankāvatāra Sūtra* the Buddha is asked for an explanation of his claim to be all the Buddhas of the past, and he responds: "I and other Tathāgatas, Arhats, Fully-Enlightened Ones are the same as regards our Dharmakāya and the signs and the minor excellencies of bodily perfection—no distinction existing among us, except that the Tathāgatas manifest varieties of forms according to the different dispositions of beings, who are to be disciplined by varieties of means." [24]

It was inevitable that the more idealistic strands of Mahāyāna, stemming from the Yogācāra school, should increasingly reduce the *Nirmānakāya* to the realm of idea, constituting a Buddhist docetism. But Mādhyamika's disavowal of either idealism or simple realism has also had its effect, and a powerful one. Tendai Buddhology today, for instance, sees particular things and persons as "real" in a dependent and transitory way, and for this school it follows that the *Nirmānakāya*-Buddha is really a man but, at the same time, is a unique expression of the Truth which, in essence, is the Reality of us all. The saying of Jesus, "I am the way, and the truth, and the life" [25] would be an admirable expression of *Nirmānakāya*. To press this fascinating analogy a little farther, Anesaki says: "The fundamental maxim of Tendai ethics is 'to put on the robes of the Tathagata, to occupy the seat of the Tathagata,' in short, to live the life of the universal self," [26] and St. Paul's most succinct expression of Christian ethics is "to me to live is Christ." [27] One should be warned, however, against drawing facile conclusions from these verbal similarities without first exploring the entire systems of which they are fragments.

Any discussion of Mahāyāna Buddhology must include at least a reference to Amida, but since he has already been examined sufficiently for our purpose, we shall add only a few additional remarks now. In traditional Buddhist thought a universe is the peculiar realm of a particular

Buddha. It is its Buddha's "field" (Skt.: *kṣetra;* Pali: *khetta*) of influence in which his merit and wisdom are available to aid its people. There are, according to some teachings, many thousands of Buddha-fields, each with its sun and moon and all the appurtenances of a standard universe. Amida is the presiding Buddha of his own *kṣetra*, but he is of incalculable importance even in *our* universe because the power of his merit enables him to promise that whoever here calls upon him in faith will find rebirth in the spotless realm of his own direct influence.

Of course such a way of thinking ignores the basic fact that there are not, in final truth, many Buddhas but one *Dharmakāya*. Yet it is a soteriologically valuable concept, for it describes in useful imagery the spiritual adventure of Buddhist faith. At the end of faith's road one discovers experientially the indivisibility of Reality and, consequently, the identity of all Buddhas—and our identity, in essence, with them.

In its speculation about the Buddha, then, we see in Mahāyāna a rich extension of basic Buddhist ideas, dictated largely by the need to bring all things into harmony with the emergent affirmation of an Absolute. But what of those lesser Wayfarers who are not yet Buddhas, at least in the fullest sense of *Nirmānakāya?*

The Bodhisattva

Theravāda Buddhism offers us the goal of Arhatship in which all passions will be overcome, and release from the cycle of birth and death will be obtained. While one man may serve as an example to others, or may offer directions for attainment of understanding, essentially each of us struggles toward the light alone.

In Mahāyāna, on the other hand, the awareness that the final truth of all is the non-duality of all leads to a different view of the ideal Buddhist. Since there is, in essence, no distinction between you and me, the transference of merit is possible from one of us to the other—or, rather, the merit already belongs to all and the concept of "transference" is only a convenient way of thinking about it at this illusory level in which we seem to be separate entities. Consequently the *Arhat* who finds his own deliverance and forsakes the birth-death realm for *Nirvāna's* passionless peace has actually not quite fully understood the nature of reality after all. In an absolutist system no one's understanding can be complete until understanding is universal and no atom of illusion remains, for what is real cannot be fragmented into that which is illumined and that which is not. It remains empirically true, of course, that one man has enjoyed a Buddhist experience of enlightenment and another has not, yet in the deepest truth what must be said is that light is overcoming darkness whenever awakening to truth occurs, but that the darkness persists and must be fully overcome.

One must think organically, not piecemeal. The truth is obscured if we are content to assume that a piece of reality has achieved its goal when a single man is enlightened. Therefore the man who truly knows the Truth will never be content until only Truth remains. On the basis of absolutism, then, Mahāyāna erects the ideal Buddhist character—not the *Arhat*, but the *bodhisattva* ("Enlightenment-Being") dedicated to the universalizing of enlightenment and willing to postpone his own final release from birth and death until that goal is achieved.

There are actually two meanings embraced by the word *bodhisattva*. The first of them, shared by both Theravāda

and Mahāyāna, refers simply to one who has determined
to attain enlightenment and is moving steadily along the
path. The other, distinctively Mahāyānist, signifies one
who himself has vowed not only to attain enlightenment
but to strive ceaselessly for the attainment of universal
Buddhahood. Even when the moment comes in which the
bodhisattva richly deserves and could obtain Nirvanic
release from rebirth, this boon will be deferred in the interest of all who suffer in illusion and must be helped. The
ideal *bodhisattva* is thus one who has achieved his awareness of absolute oneness with the Absolute and continues
to live among us, therefore, as an incarnation of Truth and
understanding. Among those modern Mahāyānists who
have abandoned the idea of rebirth or transmigration as
actual events (these have always been concepts difficult to
reconcile with other Buddhist beliefs, notably *anātman*)
the *bodhisattva* concept is also modified a little. The assumption is no longer that such a being will willingly endure rebirth after rebirth in the interests of all, but that
he continually gives himself to the task of saving all beings
and in doing so represents the continually reappearing but
essentially unborn and undying Light of Truth which is
Śūnyatā.

The Bodhisattva Vow

The Mahāyāna *bodhisattva*, then, is one who vows to
seek the enlightenment of all. This vow is a very important
part of traditional thought about the *bodhisattva* and
deserves particular (although, here, necessarily brief) attention.

The vow of the *bodhisattva* or, more properly, vows
should be made before a Buddha (*Nirmānakāya*) but

since this opportunity is rare they may be declared in the presence of other *bodhisattvas*, or by calling on the legendary "Buddhas of the Ten Directions" as witnesses. The vows mark a very serious point in a human career, since they signify that a great deal of progress has already been made along the Enlightenment Way and the attainment of the end is now to become the consuming preoccupation of the life in question.

There are typically two sections of vows, the first being quite standard, and the second being distinctive to the particular person making them. The standard vows may be roughly translated as follows:

1. Even if there is a boundless number of sentient beings, I vow to bring all of them to the Truth;
2. Even if evil passions attack me in countless number, I vow to overcome them all;
3. Even if the pathways to Truth are so numerous that they defy mastery, I vow to master all of them;
4. Enlightenment may be beyond the grasp of men, but I vow to attain it.

The third of these vows may need comment. Since the *bodhisattva* is not concerned merely to achieve an individualistic goal but to serve the interests of all beings, he must be able to deal appropriately with each person who comes to him for help. It may not suffice to offer the same teaching in the same manner to all, for the obstacles which different men confront are unique to them. There are many problems to be overcome and, consequently, many paths to the Truth but perhaps only *one* path that is in any given moment suitable for some particular person. Unless the *bodhisattva* has mastered all the possible approaches to Truth, there will therefore be someone he cannot help,

200

and this is not a situation which the *bodhisattva* finds acceptable.

As in so many things, Pure Land Buddhism has something distinctive to add to the notion of the *bodhisattva* vow. It sees the vow of every *bodhisattva* as essentially the expression of Amida's all-sufficient Vow. Consequently the Pure Land Buddhist sees himself not so much as the one who originates a vow, but as the humble vehicle through which Amida's Vow works in the world. Indeed, they do not declare themselves to be *bodhisattvas*, for they have a profound consciousness of their own inadequacy as men of a degenerate age, yet they live in order to be the hands and feet of Amida's all-availing Vow and thus perform the *bodhisattva* function without the risk of self-deluding arrogance.

If we seek an example of the distinctive, personal vowing of a *bodhisattva*, we can do no better than examine the list of affirmations allegedly made by Amida when he lived as a *bodhisattva*. According to the *Larger Sukhā-vātīvyūha Sūtra*, there were forty-eight of these special vows, the most important (for us) of which is the eighteenth:

> Upon my attainment of Buddhahood, if the beings in ten quarters who have sincere mind, serene faith, and wish to be born in my land with even ten utterances would *not* be born therein, may I not attain the highest enlightenment.[28]

The "ten quarters" is merely a conventional way of referring to the entire realm of existence including all possible Buddha-fields. The "utterances" referred to are the speaking of a traditional formula of adoration to Amida—*namu Amida Butsu*—technically referred to as the *nembu-*

tsu. Thus the meaning of this vow is that any being anywhere who in faith and sincerity calls adoringly upon
Amida may be assured of rebirth in Amida's land. There
has been long debate about the specification of "ten
utterances," some arguing that this is to be taken literally
as the required number of times the *nembutsu* must be
used in order to attain the gift of Amida's promise and
others seeing it merely as an expression indicating how
little is required other than sincerity and faith, but the
essential point is clear. It is on the strength of Amida's distinctive vows that the Pure Land sects rest their case. If
Amida made such a vow and then acquired the merit to
make it effective, his grace is now sufficient for all of us.

The Qualities of a Bodhisattva

Returning now to a consideration of the character of
bodhisattvahood, we must make it clear that the ideal
bodhisattva is indeed a person of special qualities:

> The Lord said: Here, Subhuti, someone who has set out in
> the vehicle of a Bodhisattva should produce a thought in
> this manner: "As many beings as there are in the universe
> of beings . . . I must lead to Nirvana, into that Realm
> of Nirvana which leaves nothing behind. And yet, although
> innumerable beings have thus been led to Nirvana, no
> being at all has been led to Nirvana." And why? If in a
> Bodhisattva the notion of a "being" should take place, he
> could not be called a "Bodhi-being." [29]

Now, this passage from the *Diamond Sūtra* makes it
clear that the *bodhisattva* is characterized by two qualities
which co-exist in considerable logical tension. His concern
to lead all beings to *Nirvāna* is the fruit of his great *karunā*
("compassion") which cannot rest content until there is

202   THE VAGRANT LOTUS

no suffering and no ignorance remaining. But as love drives
the *bodhisattva* to seek untiringly the salvation of all
beings, his transcendental wisdom (*prajñā*) obliges him
to know that there are no beings in need of salvation: that
the *Dharmakāya* is All! The same *Diamond Sūtra* emphasizes the *prajñā* of the *bodhisattva* when it says of him
that in him:

   (1) no perception of a self takes place, (2) no perception
   of a being, (3) no perception of a soul, (4) no perception
   of a person. Nor do these Bodhisattvas have (5) a perception of a dharma, or (6) a perception of a no-dharma. (7)
   No perception or (8) non-perception takes place in them.[30]

This means that the *bodhisattva* is no longer deceived into
believing in the substantial reality of egos, individuality,
enduring spiritual identities, or even of the Theravādin
point-instants. In fact, he no longer believes in the subject-
object antithesis that is expressed by the conventional
terminology of perception or non-perception. The unborn,
undying, undeceived *Dharmakāya* alone authentically *is*.
This is wisdom. Yet he must strive bravely for the deliverance of all beings who dwell in darkness, suffering,
and fear. As one critic says of the *bodhisattva:*

   Though aware of the nothingness of all things and of the
   ultimate irrelevance of all exertions of the spirit, he never
   ceases to work for the benefit of all sentient beings.[31]

The problem herein arises from the fact that in Mahāyāna thought the individual is taken seriously in soteriology
but not in ontology. The *bodhisattva* may, then, be said to
embody the clearest rational inconsistency of Mahāyāna:
the conviction that there are worlds to be saved when
nothing *is*, apart from the Truth.

The *bodhisattva*, of course, does not represent the end

of the Mahāyāna road. His function is relevant for that
interim before the dawning of cloudless Truth. He looks
and works for the day when all *bodhisattvas* shall have
become Buddhas, and there shall therefore be no Buddhas
at all but the indivisible Truth. *Prajñā* shall then be full,
and *karunā* shall have become redundant, for there shall
be no object, even in illusion, to love. The Wayfarers shall
have vanished and there shall be no Way, for there shall
then be no distinction between "ought" and "is"; nothing
shall be lacking and there shall be no stumbling words
clutching in futility at elusive Truth. For where there are
no distinctions, nothing needs a name and no one asks for
explanations.

NOTES

CHAPTER I. THE BUDDHA: THE MAN, THE MESSAGE,
AND THE MYTH

1. Cf. the *Sallekha Sutta* of the *Majjhima Nikāya*.
2. Walpola Rahula, *What the Buddha Taught* (Grove Press, Inc., 1962), p. 38.
3. *Digha Nikāya* II; XXII: 18.
4. *Aṅguttara Nikāya* III: 35.
5. *Digha Nikāya* II; XXII: 19.
6. *Ibid.*, II; XXII: 20.
7. *Saṃyutta Nikāya* II; XII: 1.
8. *Digha Nikāya* II; XXII: 21.
9. *Ibid.*
10. *Aṅguttara Nikāya* V: 177.
11. *Majjhima Nikāya* I: 301.
12. Much of what follows concerning the birth of the Buddha is based upon the *Avidūre Nidāna* which is available in an English translation by T. W. Rhys Davids entitled *Buddhist Birth Stories* (London: George Routledge & Sons, Ltd., n.d.), pp. 144–145.
13. *Dhammapada*, 153–154 (author's translation).
14. Bhikkhu J. Kashyap, "Origin and Expansion of Buddhism," in Kenneth W. Morgan (ed.), *The Path of the Buddha: Buddhism Interpreted by Buddhists* (The Ronald Press Co., 1956), p. 9.

15. Aśvaghosha, *Buddhacarita* XXVII: 83–86.
16. *Dīgha Nikāya* XI (freely paraphrased).

CHAPTER III. BUDDHISM: RELIGION OR PHILOSOPHY?

1. Sir Monier Monier-Williams, *Buddhism* (Macmillan and Co., 1889), p. 537.
2. Alfred North Whitehead, *Religion in the Making* (The Macmillan Company, 1927), p. 50.
3. Deut. 6:5 (RSV).
4. Erich Fromm, *Psychoanalysis and Religion* (Yale University Press, 1958), p. 21.
5. Paul Tillich, *Dynamics of Faith* (Harper & Brothers, 1958), pp. 1–2.
6. Norbert Wiener, *I Am a Mathematician* (Doubleday & Company, Inc., 1956), pp. 323–325.
7. I am indebted for many suggestions developed in the remainder of this chapter to Wilfred Cantwell Smith's provocative book *The Meaning and End of Religion* (The Macmillan Company, 1962).

CHAPTER IV. THE NATURE OF REALITY AND
THE GROUND OF VALUE

1. The Theravāda scriptures include the following materials:

A. The *Vinaya Piṭaka* ("Basket of Discipline"). This consists of three major collections:
   1. *Sutta Vibhaṅga*
      a. *Mahā-vibhaṅga*
      b. *Bhikkhunī-vibhaṅga*
   2. *Parivāra*
   3. *Khandhaka*
      a. *Mahāvagga*
      b. *Cullavagga*

B. The *Sutta Piṭaka* ("Basket of Sermons"). There are five collections contained here:
   1. *Dīgha Nikāya* ("Long Discourses")
   2. *Majjhima Nikāya* ("Middle Length Discourses")

3. *Saṃyutta Nikāya* ("Kindred Sayings")
4. *Aṅguttara Nikāya* ("Gradual Sayings")
5. *Khuddaka Nikāya* ("Short Discourses")
The *Khuddaka Nikāya* consists of fifteen books which contain some of the most expressive and important of the Pali scriptures. Its individual books are entitled:
   a. *Khuddaka Pātha*
   b. *Dhammapada*
   c. *Udāna*
   d. *Itivuttaka*
   e. *Sutta Nipāta*
   f. *Vimānavatthu*
   g. *Petavatthu*
   h. *Theragāthā*
   i. *Therīgāthā*
   j. *Jātaka*
   k. *Niddesa*
   l. *Paṭisambhidā*
   m. *Apadāna*
   n. *Buddhavaṃsa*
   o. *Cariyā Piṭaka*
C. The *Abhidhamma Pitaka* ("Basket of Exposition"). There are seven books in this collection:
   1. *Dhamma Saṅgaṇi*
   2. *Vibhaṅga*
   3. *Dhātu Kathā*
   4. *Puggala Paññatti*
   5. *Kathā Vatthu*
   6. *Yamaka*
   7. *Paṭṭhāna*

2. Cf. the *Dhātuvibhaṅga Sutta* of the *Majjhima Nikāya*.

3. Lucien Stryk (ed.), "Questions of Milinda," in *World of the Buddha: A Reader* (Doubleday & Company, Inc., Anchor Books, 1969), pp. 91–93.

4. *Saṃyutta Nikāya* III: 53.

5. The main sources for the discussion of *Āyatanas* and *Dhātus* are the first three treatises of the *Abhidhamma* work

entitled *Vibhaṅga*, the *Dhamma Saṅgaṇi*, and the *Dhātu Kathā*.

6. Lucien Stryk (ed.), "The Discourse on the Middle Path," in *World of the Buddha*, p. 286.

7. Buddhist cosmological doctrine is widely scattered, but two important and reasonably available sources are the *Dhamma Sangaṇi* (e.g., vv. 2–10) and the *Visuddhimagga* ("Path of Purification") by Bhadantācariya Buddhaghosa (e.g., Chap. XIII). The *Dīgha Nikāya*, XXVI, is also useful.

8. *Dīgha Nikāya* XXVI: 22, 23.

9. Perhaps the most accessible single source for a study of *Nirvāna* in Theravāda thought is the *Milinda Pañha*, or "Questions of Milinda" (in Stryk, ed., *World of the Buddha*), where the concept is discussed and illustrated at considerable length.

10. *Sutta Nipāta*, ed. by Lord Chalmers (London: Oxford University Press, 1932), p. 1076.

11. *Khuddaka Nikāya, Udāna* VIII: 1–3.

12. *Samyutta Nikāya* V: 437.

13. Cf. Winston L. King, *A Thousand Lives Away* (Harvard University Press, 1964), p. 98.

14. "The Heart Sutra," in *Buddhist Wisdom Books*, ed. and tr. by Edward Conze (London: George Allen & Unwin, Ltd., 1958), pp. 77–78.

15. Sir Charles N. Eliot, *Hinduism and Buddhism: An Historical Sketch* (London: Routledge & Kegan Paul, Ltd., 1962), Vol. II, p. 43.

16. *Mādhyamika Śāstra* XXIV: *Kārika* 16.

17. Yamakami Sōgen, *Systems of Buddhistic Thought* (Calcutta: University of Calcutta Press, 1912), p. 295.

18. *Ibid.*, p. 20.

19. *Ibid.*, p. 23.

20. T. R. V. Murti, *The Central Philosophy of Buddhism* (London: George Allen & Unwin, Ltd., 1955), p. 142.

21. It should be noted that throughout this chapter the terms "Vedānta" and "Vedāntic" refer not to a specific school of philosophy or religion but to a pervasive non-dualism which certainly preceded the recognized Vedānta philosophers in India.

22. *The Lankāvatāra Sūtra*, tr. by D. T. Suzuki (London:

Routledge & Kegan Paul, Ltd., 1956), Chap. 2, section LII, p. 108.
23. *Ibid.*, Chap. 2, section VI, p. 36.
24. *Ibid.*, "Sagathakam," vv. 273–278, pp. 248–249.
25. Lalmani Joshi, *Studies in the Buddhistic Culture of India* (Delhi: Motilal Banarsidass, 1967), p. 228.
26. Hiroshi Sakamoto, Otani University, Kyoto, unpublished notes.
27. Pang Chu-shih, T'ang dynasty Zen layman.

CHAPTER V. MAN AND HIS EXISTENCE

1. Quoted by Edward Conze, *Buddhist Meditation* (London: George Allen & Unwin, Ltd., 1956), pp. 63–64.
2. G. P. Malalasekera, "The Status of the Individual in Theravāda Buddhism," *Philosophy East and West*, Vol. XIV, No. 2 (July, 1964), p. 147.
3. Maha Thera U Thittila, "The Fundamental Principles of Theravāda Buddhism," in Morgan (ed.), *The Path of the Buddha*, p. 87.
4. *Saṃyutta Nikāya* III: 2, 10.
5. Malalasekera, *loc. cit.*, p. 150.
6. *Ibid.*
7. Kashyap, "Origin and Expansion of Buddhism," in Morgan (ed.), *The Path of the Buddha*, p. 24.
8. King, *A Thousand Lives Away*, p. 19.
9. L. De Hoya, "Meditation on Plato and Buddha," *The Eastern Buddhist*, Vol. VII, No. 1 (May, 1936), p. 49.
10. *Saṃyutta Nikāya* III: 104.
11. Mahāyānists, of course, would describe Theravāda's peculiar teachings as either a deviation from or an incomplete version of the Buddha's teaching—possibly a teaching he gave to less gifted or to advanced disciples to prepare them by skillful means (*upāya*) for the full Truth as discussed in Mahāyāna.
12. D. T. Suzuki, *Mysticism: Christian and Buddhist; The Eastern and Western Way* (Collier Books, 1962), p. 95.
13. Hui Neng, *The Sūtra of Hui Neng*, tr. by A. F. Price and

Wong Mou-Lam (Berkeley: Shambala Publications Ltd., 1969), pp. 11–19.

14. D. T. Suzuki, *Outlines of Mahayana Buddhism* (Schocken Books, Inc., 1963), p. 116.

15. *Ibid.*, p. 117.

16. *Ibid.*, p. 118.

17. Daiei Kaneko, "The Meaning of Salvation in the Doctrine of Pure Land Buddhism," *The Eastern Buddhist*, Vol. I, No. 1 (New Series) (September, 1965), p. 49.

18. Masao Abe, " 'Life and Death' and 'Good and Evil' in Zen," *Criterion*, Vol. 9, No. 1 (Autumn, 1969), p. 7.

CHAPTER VI. THE WAY AND THE WAYFARERS

1. Phil. 2:12–13 (NEB).

2. *The Dhammapada*, tr. by Irving Babbitt (New Directions Books, 1965), vv. 165–166.

3. Buddhaghosa, *Visuddhimagga* I:55.

4. Edward Conze, *Buddhist Thought in India: Three Phases of Buddhist Philosophy* (The University of Michigan Press, 1967), p. 64.

5. Buddhaghosa, *Visuddhimagga* I:104 f.

6. *Samyutta Nikāya* V: 199–200.

7. The subject of Buddhist meditation is dealt with in many books and we shall, for the sake of completeness, do no more than summarize it here. Readers who wish further information are referred to B. Ananda Maitreya, "Buddhism in Theravāda Countries," in Morgan (ed.), *The Path of the Buddha*, or Conze, *Buddhist Meditation*, or King, *A Thousand Lives Away*.

8. Maitreya, "Buddhism in Theravāda Countries," in Morgan (ed.), *The Path of the Buddha*, pp. 150–151.

9. C. H. S. Ward, *Buddhism*, Vol. II (London: The Epworth Press, 1952), pp. 38–39.

10. A. Berriedale Keith, *Buddhist Philosophy in India and Ceylon* (Varanasi-1: The Chowkhamba Sanskrit Series Office, 1963), p. 27.

11. *Mahāvagga* XX; I: 6–8.

12. *Dīgha Nikāya* I: 33.
13. *Ibid.*, XI (freely paraphrased).
14. Stanislav Schayer, *Mahāyāna Doctrines of Salvation*, tr. by R. T. Knight (London: Probsthain and Co., 1923), p. 18.
15. Passages quoted herein from Dōgen are taken from an unpublished translation by Hiroshi Sakamoto. The translation was designed as a basis for discussion rather than for publication and is, therefore, not in the form in which Professor Sakamoto would wish finally to present Dōgen's work to an English-speaking public. The edition of the *Shōbōgenzō* on which the translation is based is the Iwanamibunko edition of 1939, edited by Sokuo Etō. Our material occupies pages 147–157 in this text.
16. D. T. Suzuki, *A Miscellany on the Shin Teaching of Buddhism* (Kyoto: Shinshū Ōtaniha Shūmusho, 1949), p. 140.
17. Quoted by Kenshō Yokogawa, *The Other-Power* (Ube City: The Karinbunko, 1965), p. 305.
18. Kenshō Yokogawa, "Shin Buddhism as the Religion of Hearing," *The Eastern Buddhist*, Vol. VII, Nos. 3–4 (July, 1939), p. 307.
19. D. T. Suzuki, "The Shin Sect of Buddhism," *The Eastern Buddhist*, Vol. VII, Nos. 3–4 (July, 1939), p. 254.
20. Anon., *From the Shin Sect* (Kyoto: The Eastern Buddhist Society, Ōtani University, 1937), p. 42.
21. Edward Conze (tr.), *Buddhist Scriptures* (Harmondsworth: Penguin Books Ltd., 1959), p. 182.
22. The "Fo Shuo Wu-Liag-Shou-Ching," *The Eastern Buddhist*, Vol. VIII, No. 3 (Nov., 1957), p. 16.
23. Murti, *The Central Philosophy of Buddhism*, p. 225.
24. *The Laṅkāvatāra Sūtra*, tr. by D. T. Suzuki, Chap. 3, section LX, p. 123.
25. John 14: 0 (RSV).
26. Masaharu Anesaki, *History of Japanese Religion: With Special Reference to the Social and Moral Life of the Nation* (Charles E. Tuttle Co., 1963), p. 118.
27. Phil. 1: 21 (RSV).
28. Suzuki, *A Miscellany on the Shin Teaching of Buddhism*, p. 16.

212

29. "The Diamond Sūtra," tr. by Edward Conze, in *Buddhist Wisdom Books*, p. 25.

30. *Ibid.*, p. 33.

31. Heinrich Dumoulin, *A History of Zen Buddhism*, tr. from the German by Paul Peachey (Pantheon Books, Inc., 1963), p. 25.

BIBLIOGRAPHY

The following works are offered as suitable for further reading
in the history and philosophy of Buddhism. The list is far from
exhaustive and some of the works are likely to be available
only from scholarly institutions or major libraries, but all should
eventually be read by anyone who aspires to proficiency in this
subject.

ORIGINAL SOURCES

Theravāda

Buddhaghosa, Bhadantācariya, *The Path of Purification*
(*Visuddhimagga*), tr. by Bhikkhu Ñāṇamoli. Colombo: R.
Semage, 1956.
Buddhist Birth Stories (*Jataka Tales*), tr. by T. W. Rhys
Davids. London: George Routledge & Sons. Ltd., n.d.
The Dhammapada, tr. by Irving Babbitt. New Directions
Books, 1965.
Dialogues of the Buddha (*Digha Nikāya*), tr. by T. W. Rhys
Davids. 3 vols. London: Pali Text Society, 1969–1971.
Discourse on Elements (*Dhātu Kathā*), tr. by U Nārada. Lon-
don: Pali Text Society, 1962.
Middle Length Sayings (*Majjhima Nikāya*), tr. by I. B. Horner.
3 vols. London: Pali Text Society, 1967.
Woven Cadences (*Sutta Nipāta*), tr. by E. M. Hare. Oxford:
Oxford University Press, 1944.

214 BIBLIOGRAPHY

Mahāyāna

Aśvaghosha, *The Awakening of Faith,* tr. by Yoshito S. Hakeda. Columbia University Press, 1967.
Conze, Edward (ed. and tr.), *Buddhist Wisdom Books.* London: George Allen & Unwin, Ltd., 1958.
The Lankāvatāra Sūtra, tr. by D. T. Suzuki. London: Routledge & Kegan Paul, Ltd., 1956.
Masunaga, Reiho (tr.), *A Primer of Sōtō Zen* (Dōgen's *Shōbōgenzō Zuimonki*). Honolulu: East-West Center Press, 1971.
The Platform Sūtra of the Sixth Patriarch, tr. by Philip B. Yampolsky. Columbia University Press, 1967.
Saddharma-Puṇḍarika ("The Lotus of the Good Law"), tr. by H. Kern. Dover Publications, Inc., 1967.

General

Conze, Edward (ed.), *Buddhist Scriptures.* Harmondsworth: Penguin Books Ltd., 1959.
Stryk, Lucien (ed.), *World of the Buddha: A Reader.* Doubleday & Company, Inc., Anchor Books, 1969.

SECONDARY SOURCES

Theravāda

Buddhadāsa, *Toward the Truth,* ed. by Donald K. Swearer. The Westminster Press, 1971.
King, Winston L., *A Thousand Lives Away.* Harvard University Press, 1964.
Nyanatiloka, Mahathera, *Guide Through the Abhidhamma Pitaka.* Colombo: Bauddha Sāhitya Sabhā, 1957.
Rahula, Walpola, *What the Buddha Taught.* Grove Press, Inc., 1962.
Swearer, Donald K., *Buddhism in Transition.* The Westminster Press, 1972.

Mahāyāna

Bloom, Alfred, *Shinran's Gospel of Pure Grace*. The Association for Asian Studies, University of Arizona Press, 1965.

Murti, T. R. V., *The Central Philosophy of Buddhism: A Study of the Mādhyamika System*. London: George Allen & Unwin, Ltd., 1955.

Schayer, Stanislav, *Mahāyāna Doctrines of Salvation*, tr. by R. T. Knight. London: Probsthain and Co., 1923.

Suzuki, D. T., *Outlines of Mahayana Buddhism*. Schocken Books, Inc., 1963.

General

Conze, Edward, *Buddhist Thought in India: Three Phases of Buddhist Philosophy*. The University of Michigan Press, 1967.

Eliot, Sir Charles N., *Hinduism and Buddhism: An Historical Sketch*. 3 vols. London: Routledge & Kegan Paul, Ltd., 1962.

Joshi, Lalmani, *Studies in the Buddhistic Culture of India*. Delhi: Motilal Banarsidass, 1967.

Keith, A. Berriedale, *Buddhist Philosophy in India and Ceylon*. Oxford: Clarendon Press, 1923.

Kern, H., *Manual of Indian Buddhism*. Strassburg: Verlag von Karl J. Trübner, 1896.

Morgan, Kenneth W. (ed.), *The Path of the Buddha: Buddhism Interpreted by Buddhists*. The Ronald Press Co., 1956.

Pande, Govind Chandra, *Studies in the Origin of Buddhism*. Allahabad: University of Allahabad Press, 1957.

Swearer, Donald K., *Secrets of the Lotus: Studies in the Buddhist Meditation*. The Macmillan Company, 1971.

Takakusu, J., *The Essentials of Buddhist Philosophy*. Honolulu: Office Appliance Co., 1956.

Thomas, E. J., *Life of the Buddha as Legend and History*. Alfred A. Knopf, Inc., 1931.

INDEX

Abe, Masao, 11, 141
Abhidamma. See Abhidharma
Abhidhamma Piṭaka, 65
Abhidharma, 39, 72, 77, 78, 87
Absolute, 52, 56, 78, 82, 95, 98,
   99, 100–107, 110, 111, 133,
   137, 139, 148, 176–180, 182–
   183, 187, 190, 193–194, 196,
   198. See also Buddha-Nature;
   Emptiness; Suchness; Śūn-
   yatā; Void
Absolutism, 96, 100, 111, 138,
   140, 175, 181, 189, 197
Ādibuddha, 192
Age, 17, 18, 30, 125
Aggregates, 18, 19, 72. See also
   Skandha
Ālayavijñāna, 106–108, 143
Amida, 183–188, 195–201
Anāgāmin, 154
Ananda, 34, 169, 184
Anātman, 100, 129, 146, 164,
   198
Aṅguttara Nikāya, 23
Anicca, 132, 146, 164. See also
   Transience
Anutpāda. See Unborn
Aquinas, Thomas, 82, 97

Arhat, Arhats, 41, 154, 165, 171,
   172, 195, 197
Arūpa Dhātu(s), 83
Asanga, 43, 175
Asceticism, 17, 31, 172
Asoka, 39, 40, 41
Aśvaghosha, 137
Ātman, 67, 68, 100–102, 142
Attā. See Atman
Avalokita, 94
Avatamsaka Sūtra, 99, 107
Avidyā. See Ignorance
Āyatana(s), 74, 75, 76, 80, 125

Bando, Shojun, 11
Becoming, 72, 92, 98, 121–126,
   130, 134
Being(s), 52, 72, 99, 111, 134,
   141, 177, 180, 181, 189, 201,
   202
Benares, 15, 33, 35
Bhava. See Becoming
Bhikkhu(s), 18–21, 158
Bhūtatā. See Reality
Birth(s), 18, 32, 35, 79, 114,
   116, 118, 121, 123, 125, 146,
   149, 168, 169, 172, 196, 197
Bodh Gaya, 31, 35

217

Bodhi. See Enlightenment
Bodhisattva, 28, 50, 94, 175, 183, 197–203
Bodhi tree, 31, 35, 121
Brahman, 36, 102, 104, 142, 143, 191
Brahmin(s), 45, 68
Buddha, the, 15, 16, 18, 20, 22, 25, 37, 38, 46, 66, 72, 74, 88, 101, 103, 109, 114, 115, 120, 121, 124, 126, 128, 129, 130–132, 142, 145, 150, 154, 155, 158, 166–170, 172, 176, 180, 182–184, 188–194, 196, 198, 203
Buddhaghosa, 148, 156
Buddhahood, 28, 129, 171, 190, 192, 193, 198, 200
Buddha-Nature, 44, 136, 139, 176, 177, 178, 181. See also Absolute; Emptiness; Suchness; *Śūnyatā;* Void

Causal Chain. See Conditioned co-production
Cause, 32, 76, 90–92, 97, 117, 122, 123
Celebration, 60, 63
Ceylon, 46
Ch'an. See Zen
Chandragupta, 39, 44
China, 46
Christ, 25, 26, 189, 195
Christianity, 26, 50, 57, 62, 81, 184
Church, 60, 64
Citta, 188
Cittaguta, 148
Clinging, 20, 122, 125, 132, 141
Concentration, 24, 149, 153, 155, 159, 173, 174; access, 162, 163, 165; attainment,

162, 163, 164; preliminary, 162. See also Meditation
Conditioned co-production, 44, 92, 121, 134
Consciousness, 71, 73–76, 79, 83, 106, 107, 113, 123, 125, 127, 130–134, 138, 163, 169, 191
Contemplation, 23, 24
Conze, Edward, 27, 148, 159
Cosmology, 82–85
Craving, 19, 20, 56, 67, 122, 124, 132, 134, 135, 145, 165, 166, 173. See also Desire; *Trishnā*
Cunda, 34, 35

Dāna. See Giving
Death, 17–19, 32, 33, 35, 37, 55, 101, 114, 118, 121, 124–128, 130, 132, 133, 140, 141, 143, 146, 149, 162, 172, 196, 197
Deer Park, 33, 35
Democritus, 79
Dependent co-production. See Conditioned co-production
Desire(s), 18–21, 32, 83, 108, 122, 125, 126, 134, 135, 137, 172, 173. See also Craving; *Trishnā*
Detachment, 20, 24, 146–149, 153, 174
Dhamma. See *Dharma*
Dhammapada, 145
Dharma: as Absolute, 103; Asoka's, 40; definitions of, 78; as *Nirvāna,* 133; as Point-Instant, 42, 43, 79, 80, 81, 84, 86–89, 91, 92, 94, 95, 103, 107, 109, 124, 128, 133, 152, 202; as Teaching, 41, 155,

158, 174; as Truth, 116, 150,
189–190
Dharmadhātu, 96, 139
Dharmakāya, 96, 100, 103, 190–
196, 201, 202
Dhātu(s), 74, 76, 78–80, 109
Dhyāna, 163. See also Concentration; Meditation
Dīgha Nikāya, 18, 84, 168
Discipline(s), 17, 21, 38, 44,
61, 65, 88, 100, 108, 134,
135, 146, 150, 155, 158, 159,
165, 174, 182
Dōgen, 175–180
Dualism, 87, 94, 135, 136, 141,
182, 187, 197
Dukkha. See Suffering

Effect(s), 32, 76, 90–92, 109,
117, 118, 139
Ego, 68, 69, 73, 100, 101, 107,
108, 113, 117, 127, 128, 133,
139, 146, 149, 178, 182, 187,
188, 202
Eightfold Path, 21, 22, 56, 76,
146, 155, 159, 165
Emptiness, 82, 109. See also Absolute; Buddha-Nature; Suchness; Śūnyatā; Void
Enlightenment, 28, 32, 37, 63,
88, 110, 121, 125, 128, 135,
136, 146, 149–151, 155, 167,
173, 174, 177, 179–186, 193,
197–200
Eternalists, 66, 80, 101
Ethics, 54, 58, 62, 172, 173,
175, 176, 180, 195
Evil, 21–23, 32, 112, 139, 145,
146, 152, 159, 176–180, 183,
185, 186

Faith, 54, 55, 62, 63, 149–153,
158, 166, 182–188, 196, 200

Feeling(s), 24, 73, 122, 125,
138, 147
Fetters, 154, 158
Form, 71, 72, 83, 163
Fromm, Erich, 53

Gautama, 16–19, 25, 27, 31–37,
46, 56, 66–69, 73, 92, 100,
101, 119–124, 129, 130, 142,
155, 166–172, 183, 189, 193.
See also Śākyamuni
Generating Experience, 52, 53,
57–63, 151, 152
Giving, 27, 173, 174, 175
God (gods), 28–30, 33, 36, 49,
52, 54, 55, 57, 96, 98, 102,
129, 145, 167, 169, 170, 189,
191
Good, 23, 32, 114, 127, 145,
152, 179, 180, 183
Gotama. See Gautama

Heart Sūtra, 94
Heaven(s), 28, 83–85, 141, 167
Hell(s), 83, 84, 141
Hinātman, 101
Hīnayāna, 41, 93, 107, 194
Hōnen, 183
Hsüan-tsang, 44
Hui Neng, 135, 136
Hung Jen, 135, 136

Idealism, 43, 79, 80, 88, 96,
104–108, 195
Ignorance, 44, 67, 86, 108, 111,
124, 125, 132–138, 145, 154,
172, 173, 181, 182, 202
Illusion, 37, 68, 72, 75, 76, 86,
92, 98, 102, 104–107, 124,
137, 140–142, 152, 172–176,
180–182, 197, 203

Impermanence. See Anicca; Transience
Islam, 45, 50

Jain(ism), 68, 90, 91
Japan, 46, 140, 182
Jarāmarana, 125
Jataka, 28, 142
Jāti, 125
Jetavana, 119
Jhāna. See Concentration; Meditation
Jiriki, 185
Jodo Shin. See Pure Land Budhism
Judaism, 50, 81

Kakusandha, 166, 169
Kāma dhātu(s), 83
Kanishka, 41
Kapilavastu, 16
Karma, 44, 106, 115–120, 123–126, 127, 133, 134, 138–140, 149, 181, 183, 186, 187
Karunā, 191, 201, 203
Kegon, 110
Keith, A. B., 130, 131, 168
Keshin, 194
Kevaddha Sutta, 36
Khanda. See Skandha
King, Winston, 129
Kliṣṭa-Mano-Vijñāna, 107
Konagamana, 166, 169
Kśānti. See Patience
Kśetra, 84, 196
Kusinagara, 34

Lankāvatāra Sūtra, 107, 108, 194
Lotus, 15, 37, 38, 46
Lust, 19, 22, 24, 154
Luther, Martin, 54, 185

Mādhyamika, 43, 89–95, 100, 103–111, 142, 191, 193, 195
Maghada, 37, 39, 44
Mahaprajapati, 34
Mahāsanghika(s), 38
Mahātissa, 147
Mahātman, 101
Maitreya, 166
Maitreyanatha, 43
Majjhima Nikāya, 21, 87, 130
Malalasekera, G. P., 114
Manas, 73–76, 107, 108, 122
Mara, 32, 33, 130, 131
Maurya, 39, 41
Maya. See Illusion
Maya, Queen, 28
Meditation, 23, 24, 27, 28, 32, 50, 93, 149, 155, 159, 162–166, 174. See also Concentration
Merit-transference, 181–184, 197
Metempsychosis, 127
Milinda, King, 41, 69
Milinda Pañha, 41, 69
Mind, 22, 24, 28, 32, 93, 107, 109, 110, 122, 123, 127, 135, 142, 148, 149, 156, 157, 160, 162, 176, 177, 179, 200
Mind-Only, 108, 109
Mindful(ness), 116, 117, 149, 152, 153, 162
Missionary, 33, 39
Monier-Williams, Monier, 49
Monism, 66, 80, 92, 103–104, 191
Monk(s), 30–39, 65, 69, 148, 149, 158
Morality, 27, 40, 49, 155, 173, 174. See also Sila
Murti, T. R. V., 194
Myth, 15, 25, 26, 58, 60, 63
Nāgārjuna, 27, 43, 82, 97, 175

Nāgasena, 69, 70, 71
Nālandā, 44
Nāmarūpa, 122, 123, 125
Nembutsu, 200–201
Nepal, 15, 46
Nibbāna. See Nirvāna
Nihilism, 66, 80, 92, 93, 101, 105
Nirmānakāya, 190, 191, 193, 194–198
Nirvāna, 33, 35, 40, 42, 44, 56, 62, 80, 83, 85–88, 109, 111, 112, 128, 130–133, 143, 148, 154, 159, 160, 163, 164, 167, 171, 191, 197, 201
Non-Returner. See Anāgāmin
Nuns, 34, 157

Ojin, 194
Once-Returner. See Sakadāgāmin
One-pointedness, 24, 149
Otani University, 176

Pacceka Buddhas, 166, 167, 171
Pain, 18, 32, 34, 83, 114, 133
Paññā. See Prajñā
Pannadhika Buddhas, 166
Parināmana. See Merit-transference
Parinirvāna, 37, 133
Parivarta. See Merit-transference
Pasenadi, 119
Patience, 27, 173, 174
Pātimokkha, 158
Peace, 17, 33, 40, 111, 112, 132, 182
Perfections, 27
Phassa. See Sparsha
Philosophy, 17, 25, 26, 49–51, 54, 59, 63, 64, 73, 78, 82, 85,

89, 93, 103, 137, 150–152, 168, 172, 179
Platform Sūtra, 135
Plato, 127
Pluralism, 28, 80, 87, 92, 96, 194
Prajñā, 103, 155, 165, 166, 174, 191, 201, 203. See also Wisdom
Predispositions. See Saṃskāra
Pure Land Buddhism, 182–188, 193, 200, 201
Pushya, 28

Rahula, 17
Rahula, Walpola, 18
Realism, 80, 105, 195
Reality, 18, 42, 43, 56, 78, 79, 82, 92, 94–96, 100, 104, 108–112, 133, 135, 136, 141–143, 176–181, 190–192, 195–197, 202
Rebirth(s), 19, 20, 126, 132, 143, 184, 185, 196, 198, 201
Religion, 17, 26, 44, 49–64, 168
Right Action, 21, 22, 155
Right Attentiveness, 21, 23, 159
Right Concentration, 21, 24, 159
Right Effort, 21, 23, 159
Right Livelihood, 21, 23, 155
Right Mindedness, 21, 22, 165
Right Speech, 21, 22, 155
Right Understanding, 21, 22, 165
Ritual(s), 17, 60, 63, 64
Rūpa. See Form
Rūpa dhātu(s), 83

Sacca, 18
Sakadāgāmin, 154
Sakamoto, Hiroshi, 11, 175, 179
Śakya, 16, 28

222

Śākyamuni, 182, 184. See also Gautama
Salvation, 35, 63, 128, 182, 184, 185, 187, 201
Samādhi, 155, 159. See also Concentration; Meditation
Samatā, 96
Samatha, 160, 164. See also Tranquillity
Sambhogakāya, 190–193
Saṃjña, 73
Saṃkhata, 18
Sāmkhya, 90
Saṃsāra, 111, 112, 143, 172, 191
Saṃskāra, 73, 123, 125
Saṃyutta Nikāya, 119, 130, 149
Sangha, 38, 150, 155, 158
Sankhāra. See Saṃskāra
Sañña. See Samjña
Sati, 130
Satyatā, 96
Sautrantika(s), 106
Sāvatthi, 119, 120
Schayer, Stanislav, 171
Science, 61
Scripture(s), 16, 17, 26, 27, 34, 38, 41, 44, 63, 65, 72, 86, 109, 121, 168, 170, 176. List of, 206–207
Self, 24, 67–74, 87, 96, 100–102, 107–108, 112–114, 124, 129, 132, 133, 139, 140, 146, 148, 154, 164, 178, 180, 183, 185, 187, 188, 202
Selfhood, 24, 71, 75, 76, 86, 101, 180
Sex, 156, 157
Shen Hsiu, 135, 136
Shingon, 193
Shinran, 182–186
Shōbōgenzō, 175
Siddhartha, 16, 17, 28, 29, 30

Sīla, 155–159, 173–174, 180, 188. See also Morality
Śiva, 45, 168
Skandha(s), 19, 72, 78–80, 94, 95, 100, 103, 108, 109, 113, 123, 148. See also Aggregates
Sōgen, Yamakami, 101
Sotāpanna, 154
Soteriology, 180, 181, 196, 202
Soul, 68, 71, 100, 101, 113, 127, 128, 129, 131, 202
Sparsha, 125
Sravasti, 34
Stealing, 22, 174
Stream-Entrant. See Sotāpanna
Stupa, 168
Subjectivity, 67, 76, 77, 108, 178
Subjects for contemplation, 160–162
Substance, 72, 79, 94, 98, 113, 124, 131, 142
Suchness, 98, 103, 111, 137, 138, 141–143, 184, 187. See also Absolute; Buddha-Nature; Emptiness; Śūnyatā; Void
Suddhadhika Buddha, 166
Suddhodana, King, 28, 29, 30
Suffering(s), 17–21, 32, 44, 55, 56, 66, 67, 83, 85, 101, 108, 111–115, 123, 126, 136, 146, 149, 164, 172, 202
Sukhāvātivyūha Sūtra, 184, 200
Śūnyatā, 94–105,109–111, 133, 136–143, 176, 181, 188, 190, 191, 198. See also Absolute; Buddha-Nature; Emptiness; Suchness; Void
Sutta Piṭaka, 65
Suzuki, D. T., 108, 111, 134, 137, 186
Svabhāva, 97
Svabhāvakāya, 96

Tanhā. See Craving; *Trishnā*
Tannishō, 186
Tariki, 185
Tathāgata, 149, 195
Tathatā, 96
Tendai, 110, 195
Thittila, Maha Thera U, 117, 119
Threefold Discipline, 146, 154, 155, 165, 182
Tibet, 46, 192
Tipiṭaka, 65
Trance(s), 28, 30, 35, 62, 66, 83, 153, 163, 174, 192
Tranquillity, 15, 153, 159, 160, 162, 163
Transcendence, 51–54, 57, 59, 62, 63, 113, 151, 184, 191, 193
Transience, 17, 20, 23, 24, 38, 42, 67, 71, 79, 80, 88, 111, 114, 124, 125, 137, 143, 148, 174, 176. See also *Anicca*
Transmigration, 44, 126, 127, 129, 131, 133, 140, 141, 142, 198
Trikāya, 189, 190, 194
Trishnā, 122, 125, 134, 135. See also Craving
Truth, 16, 18, 19–25, 32, 46, 51, 52, 56, 57, 66, 67, 86, 91, 95, 96, 99, 100, 102–105, 108–110, 112, 114, 116, 121, 125, 131, 135–138, 143, 144, 146, 148, 150, 151, 153, 164, 165, 167, 173, 175–182, 189–192, 195, 197–199, 202, 203
Truths, Four Noble, 18, 21, 24, 56, 165

Ultimate, 15, 177, 178, 184, 190–193

Unborn, 15, 87, 96, 141, 177–179, 184, 198, 202
Upādāna. See Clinging
Upanishads, 58

Vairocana-Buddha, 192
Value(s), 51, 53, 55, 60, 61, 63, 88, 111, 112, 122, 147, 152, 180
Vasubandhu, 43, 175
Vedanā. See Feelings
Vigor, 27, 28, 149, 152, 173, 174
Vijñāna. See Consciousness
Vijñānavāda. See *Yogācāra*
Vinaya Piṭaka, 65, 158
Vipassanā, 160, 164, 165, 166
Viriyadhika Buddhas, 166
Virtue(s), 149, 151, 153, 155, 173, 175
Vishnu, 45, 168
Visuddhimagga, 147, 148
Void, 62, 94–100, 103, 107, 110, 112, 136, 139–141, 180, 188–194. See also Absolute; Buddha-Nature; Emptiness; Suchness; *Śūnyatā*
Vow(s), 32, 198, 199, 200, 201; Amida's, 183, 186, 200, 201

Wiener, Norbert, 55, 56
Wisdom, 27, 94, 103, 117, 149, 153, 155, 165, 166, 173–175, 196, 202

Yasodhara, 17
Yogācāra, 43, 89, 104–111, 143, 193, 195
Yokogawa, Konshō, 185

Zen, 62, 110, 135, 141, 188